The Orphan Gospels

The Orphan Gospels

Reflections on orphan care & ministry
to the poor

Shelley Jean

with *Karen Lacey & Douglas Glenn Clark*

PAPILLON

PAPILLON PRESS

The Orphan Gospels
Reflections on Orphan Care & Ministry to the Poor
Copyright © 2019 by Shelley Jean. All rights reserved.

FIRST EDITION

Published by Papillon Press.
ISBN: 978-1-7923-1768-2

Contents

Foreword by Kathy Brooks

Founder of 2nd Story Goods and Much Ministries

The Sacred Art of Work

We grew into the idea of the transformative power of work years before we found our way to Haiti. It seems that whether we are talking about people who find themselves homeless in Western Canada or people battling addictions in the Southeast U.S., the same truths hold. People need to be nurtured and needed. We need to know that we are a part of something bigger than ourselves, not "helped" and left on the edges as an outsider or "other." As we all know, edges are dangerous places to try to live and raise a family.

This happens two ways:

1. The belonging to a new community
2. The establishing of a new story of self

Life-giving jobs through business can do both of these things.

A New Community

As primarily social creatures, we are all in search of our tribe. Enter the Sacred Art of Work! A healthy, vibrant company where real work is done can become that for us. This is a place where we are known, respected, and needed. This is a tribe worth showing up for each day.

Great businesses create great tribes. These are places where people become the best version of themselves because they are positioned to succeed, and they have mentors committed to this process.

The poor and marginalized who begin to work in productive companies most often find people who think differently and model new behavior. This is critical to break cycles of systemic poverty!

Establishing a new story of self

We define ourselves by what we spend our time doing. Women who had been bought and sold as sex workers thought themselves to be only that—destructive and ashamed. When we brought them into our enterprise and put them in charge of growing flowers and mixing healthy soil, watering and nurturing seeds, over time they began to know themselves as growers of good things. When introduced as a member of our staff, they would hold their head up high and say, "I am a gardener, a grower in the greenhouse." The work itself redefined their story, what they knew to be true about themselves.

Productive work is so crucial to the equation of freedom and justice and the story that gets passed down generation to generation. How proud the kids in our local school are to tell their teacher that their mom is one of the jewelry makers in the community. How proud fathers are to come home with decent paychecks each week.

The gospel is good news to the poor and it has real legs. It looks like something on the ground. The words of the kingdom are important but without the work they can become powerless. I am convinced that "on earth as it is in Heaven" looks like environments where transformation takes place. Business is a placeholder for the Sacred Art of Work. I am wholeheartedly committed to it!

REVIEWS FROM SHELLEY'S PREVIOUS BOOK:
SHELLEY IN HAITI

Shelley's story is brutally honest, heartbreaking, hopeful and real. Having been connected with Haiti for seventeen years I have learned about the hopelessness and "one step forward, twenty steps backward" that are constants in Haiti and have seen and been part of the band-aid approaches to these constants. Shelley threw out the band-aid box and created a long-lasting, personalized, and empowering solution to the cycle of misery so prevalent in this beautiful country. Throughout her book she puts faces on "those poor Haitians" and we see them as people with dreams, hopes, and love for their children mirroring our own. I have been purchasing and gifting Papillon products for years and each ornament, necklace, and piece of art is top quality. I love seeing the reactions of my friends and family members as they see and hold their gift, but telling them how these precious items give hope and dignity to the artisans is the ultimate gift.

—Nancy Wagner

What an amazing read! A perfect combination of truth and compassion concerning Haiti and the orphan crisis. Full of both the joys and hardships of working with the poor in Haiti through her own personal stories. Definitely a MUST READ! Don't forget your tissues. I read it in about five hours as I couldn't put it down. Each story leaving you wanting more.

—Cami Franklin

Such an amazing and inspiring story! Shelley tells her experiences in a real and raw way, in this really captivating story. I loved how inspiring and hopeful her story is. I love seeing how she is changing the landscape of poverty in Haiti. This book is an amazing story and a great read!

—Becky Schneider

Author's Note

$\mathcal{H}$ere I am. A woman born entrenched in the evangelical Christian community. I was raised to know all the answers and be ready to give an account. I spent years playing Bible Bingo in Vacation Bible School and was the Bible Baseball champ every time I played. I memorized John 3:16 along with 400 other key verses, poured the communion grape juice, and broke the crackers as a middle schooler. By high school, I was proud to oversee the worship slide projector, knowing all the songs by heart. (Those of you who grew up in that world hear where I am coming from.)

Yet those who know me best have seen my own faith falter as I wrestled with what I have seen in Haiti over the years and tried to make sense of it all. Desperate poverty, injustice, and chronic pain have made me question so much of what I have known to be unalterable truths. One issue I have wrestled with because of my upbringing is the notion that the mission of Christianity *is primarily to make converts*. It seemed to be the undeniable emphasis of evangelical Christianity. Heaven is our focus and chief concern.

But as an adult, reading the scripture with a new lens on poverty issues, my heart is drawn to the message of Christ that resonates deeply in the context of poverty. The poor mattered deeply to Jesus. A part of me must believe — and I do believe, as scripture backs it up — that God cares deeply about our *present* lives and our *current* struggles on planet earth *in this very moment.* He cares about our pain and our suffering. *He cares about heaven on earth.*

The strong evangelical emphasis of my upbringing had me wanting to go to the ends of the earth to reach all people to know the name of Jesus. It is largely assumed by many evangelical churches in America that most foreign countries, Haiti included, fall into that category of "unreached" peoples simply because they are foreign. This common misconception suggests that America is the "Christian nation," and all other countries are students of the faith to American Christian missionaries. However, I think it is fair to say that the world we evangelicals grew up in has in many ways flip-flopped. America is not "churched" in the way it once was and while the pews sit vacant in churches all over our country, many places in Africa, Korea, and elsewhere in the world are experiencing revivals and growth of the Christian faith in record numbers. There is no doubt that we in America have ample resources to offer, and that might indeed be our first calling (to be generous with our resources and influence), but those impoverished populations bring exceptional value by challenging our faith and assumptions about God and the world at large. Their faith in the midst of mind-blowing setbacks, struggles, and pain leaves us with something real to study and learn from. I struggle with catch-all phrases that I grew up with.

"He won't give you anything you can't handle."

"It's all for God's glory."

"He will always protect and provide."

Each of these statements has me baffled. Things I never questioned before my encounters with dire poverty now have my world upside-down.

I have found the faith of the poor to be beyond my own understanding. Their simple and humble faith is extraordinary in spite of their plentiful challenges. I have indeed learned so much about faith from my Haitian friends.

Another thing I took for granted before my time in Haiti is the way we as evangelicals do "world missions." Those of us who believe in being *Jesus followers* understand that mission work extends beyond conversion experiences, and understand also that it includes a mandate to care for the poor, yet we have become reckless in the way we handle caring for the poor — and even worse, in how we care for the orphan. If proselytizing is the evangelical foundation, then "caring for widows and orphans in their distress" has become a second new slogan for the evangelical Christian. However, the way that this plays out in Haiti (and other vulnerable countries) must be examined. I have seen and witnessed orphanage institutions funded by well-meaning churches in America that have the direct opposite effect of what the church intended. Too often, we inadvertently contribute to child abandonment, abuse, and the destruction of families in the name of following Jesus. Our church has become the Pied Piper, luring children away from their families into orphanages with a promise of food and education, and then falling miserably short of those promises over time. A child is an eighteen-year (or more) commitment. Opening an orphanage is a lifelong commitment to quality care for a child until they are successful adults or get adopted. And yet that is not what we are seeing on the ground in Haiti and other countries.

To those who are charitable and have given sacrificially over the years, this truth may sting. It certainly did for me. We all want to believe that the money we send in good faith is actually helping. And if it isn't, we don't know what to do to rectify the situation. It feels like a no-win situation. Do we quit being generous? Do we stop supporting a ministry that we have invested years into? How is that a good outcome for anybody?

I certainly don't have all the answers, but I do know that my own epiphany happened after years of witnessing so-called benevolent orphanage networks systematically fail children. I saw long-term solutions that might offer a way out for the poor. My heart fell in love with the mothers losing their children to poverty.

The Orphan Gospels is a cry to the church to start hearing and understanding the tears of the poor a little more clearly. To try to understand their unique situations and challenges so that we can truly bring "good news to the poor."

The Bible is clear and bold about the mandate to care for the poor. It is also harsh about the consequences of ignoring the responsibility.

Consequence must have been on the mind of author and activist Dorothy Day, author of *The Reckless Way of Love: Notes on Following Jesus,* whose view of dedicating her life to serving the poor is its own singular gospel:

"The mystery of the poor is this: That they are Jesus, and whatever you do for them you do to him."

If we don't do better, wonderful people and their potential contributions to the kingdom will be lost. There is nothing more tragic than seeing well-meaning and generous people send money to something that brings hurt rather than healing. *We must care enough to get it right.* When we do, we answer the call etched into our hearts from the day new life was breathed into us. We become more and more like our Maker. The gospel of Jesus Christ mandates care for the "least of these." In these pages, I reveal how my own passion for the poor as a Christ follower impacts my personal and business decisions and how you might allow them to work in your heart, too, whether in missions abroad or at home.

Shelley Jean

The Poor Will Always Be with You: Understanding Systemic Poverty

Luke 6:20
"Blessed are you who are poor for yours is
the kingdom of Heaven."

*A*t the epicenter of poverty, we find the orphan. A child. A helpless and vulnerable child, who through no fault of his or her own is alone in this world. It is certainly a passion of the Gospels to tend to the needs of orphans and other vulnerable people. Scripture backs this up with its numerous mandates to care for the widows, orphans, and poor. There is no movement or religion or government that would stand against it. Seeing children suffer moves any decent person — no matter what religion, race, or creed.

Orphan care is, simply put, a holy practice that lands us as Christ followers in a place where we can almost hear His heartbeat.

The question then is HOW to go about it. We all can wake up in the morning in our comfortable first world lives and cringe and still think to ourselves, "I don't know *how* to care for the poor. What can I do to really help?"

Maybe we search for an internet site and send money to a reputable charity or give money to our local church. But do we really know if we are helping? Most of us are just too far removed from deep poverty to know true impact. And some of us are too busy to take the time to figure it out. Nonetheless, an internet click to send money renders our conscience cleared. We know we are called to care, and our pocketbooks prove we do. But our hands may never have touched the wounds of poverty or seen any true relief. Do we dare do due diligence and dig deeper? Most of us never will. But the fact that you are reading this book makes me believe that *YOU* will and that you want your charity and volunteer efforts to have an impact. You want to do better and are looking for ways to find real solutions.

* * *

The questions have to be asked: What is an orphan? How did they get to be orphans? Are they true orphans? Are they poverty orphans? What's the difference? Who is responsible for them? Will my donations really help? What happens when they grow up?

Perhaps the most important question, if we dare ask it, follows next in this line of thinking, *How could we prevent them from ever becoming orphans in the first place?*

We might even ask how we can have an impact on systemic poverty, a clear catalyst to the orphan crisis. The words of Jesus haunt us: "The poor will always be with you." Is it a curse? Is there really no end to poverty? Could we dare to dream that Jesus might not have meant it in the way we hear it? Is it possible, even probable, given His nature, that He would want them to *flourish* the same as we do?

Maybe you don't feel like you are flourishing. Maybe you have your own struggles and feel overwhelmed by your own daily challenges. While I empathize and know how real all of our pain is, I can also assure you that you are flourishing in ways that the poor could never dream of. We live in a society with water fountains and food banks, public education, medical care, and plumbing even for the poorest of us in a first world country. Again, I don't want to discount each person's struggles and pain, but we have truly won the lottery by our birthplace and time in a way that very few genera-tions in the history of the world have been privy to.

The age-old answer to the systemic problems of poverty in poor communities abroad has most often been to build orphanag-es. More and more we are finding that this solution is not meeting the needs of the poor in the way we intended and in certain circum-stances may be contributing to more problems.

This book wrestles with grey areas of poverty and orphan care. It brings up challenges that those of us who have never in-teracted with the poor may be unaware of. Often the churches and individuals funding and making the decisions about how best to care for orphans have little hands-on experience working with them. Unfortunately, a week-long trip to hold babies does not make one an expert in solving the orphan crisis. My intention is to shed light on the complexities that we, who have almost always had our needs met, may be unaware of. To put it bluntly, we are often naïve people with big hearts.

The good news is that we can do better. We can always strive to learn more, understand more, listen more, and change accord-ingly so that we have the most impact on the pain we are trying to alleviate.

This book may be challenging. I hope it is. I want you to be challenged in the way I have been while working with the poor. But I also hope that, in the end, the questions raised will help us do a better job of loving people. My prayer is that it will indeed be a book that inspires change in those working with the poor *and that it does become good news to orphans everywhere.*

1. The Supermarket Inquisition

$\mathcal{S}$tanding in line at the grocery store with my four kids can create attention and curiosity. Up until recently, the kids spent most, if not all the year in Haiti. Upon our return to the United States, a first stop was usually to the local grocery store or Costco to splurge on cereal, milk, cheese, and chocolate, things that were luxuries to us in Haiti.

The cashier is friendly, commenting on each product she scans, and questioning my children about school and other topics. We stick out. We are a mixed-race family of four kids, two of whom are Haitian. It's obvious that I have most likely adopted, but because it is taboo to ask the question directly, people often try to make small talk to indirectly figure out the situation. Questions range between subtle and blunt.

"Oh, so many kids! Do you run a daycare?"

"No." I smile politely.

"Wow! Are they all yours?"

"Yes. Yes, they are. All mine." I smile again.

Maybe they think they will hurt my kids' feelings, as if they haven't noticed the differences themselves. My son Jackson admits that he is embarrassed from time to time at school that we don't match. He gets tired of explaining it to his friends.

Sometimes curious people like the cashier pry answers from my children. On this particular day, my sweet daughter Ember piped up, "We just started school!"

"Wow! What grade are you in?" asked the smiley cashier as the scanner chimed the cost of a box of cereal, which was then handed to the boy with braces who was bagging our groceries.

"I'm in the second grade now. I was in the first laaaast year!" Ember turns to me. "Mom, can we get some M&M's or Chiclets? We NEVER get these at home." The impulse snack rack is working its magic on my kids. I look down at their pleading eyes, then turn when I hear the cashier question us further. "At home? Are you here on vacation? Where do you all live?" The cashier was baited and hooked. Before my kids could answer ahead of me, I blurt out, "The Caribbean."

"Oh, wow!" The cashier is enthusiastic. "That must be paradise to live in the Caribbean. Like living on vacation." Her eyes sparkle.

I nod and smile.

If only she knew.

"Yeah, it's nice. Summer all year long." I try to sound optimistic, and I quickly pay, collect my receipt, and hurry my cart out of the store with my four children in tow. Ember runs up and grabs my hand. "Mom! What's the Cuh=rib=EE-an?"

"Never mind. It's just the area where Haiti is."

"Why didn't you just say Haiti? I'm Haitian." She scrunches her nose up at me.

"Yes, you are." I can never get enough of her beautiful brown skin and big round eyes. "You are my Haitian princess. But I just didn't want to get into a conversation about Haiti right now. We have errands to run."

Ember quickly climbs into the car so she won't be stuck sitting in the middle seat, while in my mind I count the many times I had generalized my home by saying "the Caribbean." It began as a survival tactic after many complicated and sometimes frustrating conversations that began after I casually mentioned "I live in Haiti" or "I'm going to Haiti" or "I have spent almost a decade in Haiti." Often these statements were met with concerned, wrinkled-up foreheads and replies of unanswerable questions that became all too predictable:

"Didn't they have that earthquake there a few years back? Are things any better?"

"What happened to all the aid money? The Red Cross is so crooked!"

"Oh, why is that country so poor? Why can't they ever get back on their feet?"

"When I am ready, I want to adopt from Haiti too. How hard is it to bring a baby home?"

And, finally, my least favorite, *"Don't they know about birth control? Why do they have so many kids anyway?"*

Questions like these render me speechless, stuttering for where to begin. The answers are so complex and overwhelming — even for me, someone considered to be "in the know" about the Haitian economy, political system, and social mores. This is precisely why I dodged the friendly curiosity of the grocery store clerk and so many other conversations like it. Haiti cannot be adequately explained as the checkout scanner beeps my purchases of milk and cheese. Not only do I usually not have the time, but quite frankly, many people don't really want to know. So I spare them.But the questions are still out there, dangling for the few who are curious and blessed enough to be hit with a passion for the poor. A few years back in 2017, the weather reports served to re-awaken the inquisition. Hurricane Irma, one of the most forceful Atlantic Ocean storms ever recorded, began to threaten the Caribbean. The meteorological maps projecting her path were terrifying. As Irma roared toward Haiti it looked like she was ready to deal another critical blow to the island.

The fact that I was safely in America with my family now, with food on the table, far from the heavy winds, brought me no peace. It did the reverse. For the last decade when hurricanes threatened, I had been in Haiti, poised to help. This time I was a helpless observer, glued to my television, hoping and praying the nation and people (my friends) I loved who were in the direct path of danger would be spared.

Unfortunately, this wasn't a one-of-a-kind catastrophe, but the continuation of an historic, ubiquitous pattern of violent weather, political strife, and acts of nature that exacerbate cycles of poverty and self-defeating mindsets that have hammered the Haitian psyche for decades.

Why can't Haiti get better? Why isn't it getting any better?

The answers are embedded in a long history of deeply disturbing events.

2. Haiti 101:
A Story of Habitual Crisis

*L*et's start with Christopher Columbus. He discovered the "New World" when he landed on the northern shores of what is now called Haiti. He named the Island Hispaniola and found it full of natives known as the Tainos. Shortly after his arrival the vast majority were dead — victims of disease and cruelty. It is a common thread that seems to follow in the wake of exploration and colonization.

In the late 1600s, the French took over the western part of Hispaniola from Spain and named it Haiti, or Land of Mountains. Most people don't know about the beauty of the Haitian mountains, which are truly breathtaking. I wish the news and media would show more of the stunning views that are Haiti's mountains and beaches, rather than the abject poverty that seems to occupy the screens. I have traveled to more than thirty countries and can honestly say that the beauty I have seen in Haiti rivals many of the well-known tourist destinations of the world. It is an undiscovered gem.

The French colonists brought slaves to Haiti from West and Central Africa, from Senegal and the Congo. The impact of slavery on a culture is easy to speculate about but hard to talk about candidly (especially for me, a privileged white woman) because it is such a loaded subject.

To this day the ramifications of slavery have left scars on the hearts of Haitians. The dynamics of abuse, poverty, the misuse of power, and fatherlessness are a continued burden for the people who have been raised under the effects of ancestral slavery. Historic slavery is certainly a major player in systemic poverty. Physical freedom comes much more easily than the emotional and economic recovery for those who have been subjected to this kind of abuse. It takes generations to recover. We can see this not only in Haiti, but also in the modern-day struggles of African American communities in North and South America. The scars of slavery carry on generation after generation. These people are faced with a burden and a battle that those of us who have been more historically privileged will never know. (I pray that we will be humble enough to acknowledge our privilege and admit that we are very naïve to the struggle and have so much to learn.)

In 1801, a former slave turned militant leader, Toussaint Louverture, rose up in resistance against the French and led his people in the world's first black slave rebellion to successfully gain independence.

Most historical accounts I have read about this monumental accomplishment focus on the heavy bloodshed and the Vodou-led uprising that was the catalyst for the overthrow. From a Christian perspective, it is sometimes used to minimize the accomplishment (as if anything in our own history of war and bloodshed is somehow more justified). Regardless of the perspective on how they gained their independence, it is important to remember that none of us were created to be enslaved, and this slave-ridden past shows the strength, resilience, and determination of the Haitian people. This is the same resilience I see today in my Haitian friends, who despite so much being stacked against them, carry on, and who want so badly to rise up and overcome. I am proud to tell my Haitian children that they are descendants of a line of people who wrestled with the shackles of slavery *and won.*

Despite this intrinsic strength within Haitians, when I look at Haiti today, I see a land dependent on outside aid from nations, charities, and individuals. It makes me long for a new uprising of strong Haitian men and women who will lead their people to freedom and prosperity not with bloodshed and turmoil, but with kindness, determination, justice, and innovation as their battle cry. This is my prayer for Haiti.

Despite the slave rebellion and promise of autonomy, the last 200 years of Haitian history have been filled with (in no particular order) injustice, assassinations, corruption, a string of dictators, threats of war by France, sanctions by France, an invasion and long-term control by the U.S., the dictatorship of François "Papa Doc" Duvalier, which his son Jean-Claude "Baby Doc" Duvalier continued until he was removed by a 1986 coup, the ongoing presence of United Nations forces, and political instability that seems habitual. This violent convergence of nations, motivations, and power-grabbing greed have made this country a political soap opera.

Now, add to that serial natural disasters like the historic 2010 earthquake and an ongoing stream of hurricanes and devastating tropical storms. Haiti is geographically located in the middle of a freeway for climatic adversities. Every fall, when hurricane season rolls around, I cringe with each projection that comes forth. Haiti seems to always be sitting in the middle of the path of a hurricane. Unfortunately, small masses of land are not mobile. They can't duck or swerve, speed up or slow down. And the people can't just build their houses elsewhere. They have nowhere to go. During my decade in Haiti I can't remember one year when we weren't praying for one hurricane or another to miss us. Several did not. But the ramifications of a direct hit, though they barely make the news in the U.S., is every bit as devastating as Irma and Harvey, or Katrina.

Over the centuries, occupying nations, corrupt governments, and natural disasters as common as national holidays, all painted over a background of the roots of slavery, have made it unimaginably difficult for the Haitian people to create a first world quality of life in their country. The inability to progress due to all the obstacles I've defined, and which most of us outside Haiti will never experience, is enough to keep any country poor and oppressed.

Thinking back on the grocery store cashier who was so thrilled about my "vacation" lifestyle in the Caribbean, and the countless other people whose queries I have evaded, it's no wonder I dodge their curiosity. Correcting assumptions can be exhausting. More to the point, in Haiti's case, things don't get back to normal once the rain and wind stop. Why? Because "normal" by our definitions has never had time to establish itself.

Corrupt government officials and ongoing foreign occupation aside, let's just look at what happens after a hurricane. The devastating loss of life alone is hard to imagine, but the hurricanes also kill the agricultural lifeline that the trees and the crops offer.

But doesn't that happen everywhere in the world when disaster strikes?

Yes, many agricultural regions suffer. The difference is that Haiti's countryside has for years been devastated and deforested by the needs of the people themselves, who must harvest trees to burn for charcoal to cook their meals. That shiny gas range oven in our kitchen is far out of the reach of most Haitian families. They must instead forage for wood to turn into charcoal to burn inside their mud huts and tin shacks. This convergence of storm damage with deforestation has created a wasteland landscape with little buffer to protect crops from harsh wind, rain, and flooding.

So, when people in the grocery store line ask why Haiti can't get back on its feet, just one of many reasons is that it takes years for trees to grow back and for many crops to mature. But this will only happen if they're not assaulted in the meantime by other hurricanes. In 2016, a major storm hit southern Haiti and wiped out crops that were a food source for thousands of Haitians. Years later, the area has not yet recovered, and malnutrition is rampant. And the storms keep coming.

It seems like everything is always one step forward and two steps back.

"Is it any better than before the earthquake?" I get asked in a casual conversation with someone I have just met.

I think hard. Some things have changed. More roads. The last president made huge attempts to stimulate the economy of Haiti with his *"Haiti is Open for Business"* slogan, but honestly, I have to say, not really. The problems are so deep-rooted, and the solutions are so shallow-rooted, that a few years is simply not enough time to amend centuries of damage. Even the post-earthquake influx of millions were but a band-aid to the gaping wound that Haiti is suffering from.

Recently, a fickle Hurricane Irma missed a direct hit on Haiti, bounced off other islands, and headed north, eventually smashing into Florida. Then Hurricane Maria appeared and was re-directed somewhat by the mid-Atlantic cyclone, Hurricane Jose.

Back in Haiti we rejoiced that the island had not been badly hit — then watched the dominoes begin to fall.

The storm caused thousands of flights to be cancelled for several weeks, and that alone devastated many small business owners, including my Papillon Marketplace. No airplanes meant no tourists and missionaries who feed the local economy. During that time, we lost about $40,000 in sales from our artisanal products and café, where visitors can buy food and beverages before visiting our artisans at work. This hit on our artisans was hard.

Given the drop in sales, I was forced to reduce full-time artisans' work schedules to part-time. The ramifications were painful to watch. So many of my hard-working employees who had begun to enjoy a steady wage found themselves struggling, again, just to feed their kids and send them to school. Suffering inside our hearts and souls cannot be filmed, but it is as real as a house being submerged six feet underwater.

Ask me again: Why can't Haiti get on its feet and move forward?

The horrifying earthquake of 2010 reminded us in no uncertain terms that a significant fault line runs through the capital city of Port Au Prince. Another earthquake, they say, is imminent. Buildings that the poor raise with their own hands are not constructed to withstand hurricanes and earthquakes. When devastation hits Haiti, its people literally lose everything. Again and again. Not only possessions, but also their food sources and economies. As a result, food must continue to be imported to keep people alive. Meanwhile, there is an ongoing shortage of what is left to export that could create a national income. Common sense tells us that if we exist only as buyers and simultaneously have nothing to sell, we'll go bankrupt.

That is Haiti. Bankrupt for decades.

By now, hopefully you're starting to understand why.

Tragically, it doesn't stop with slavery, colonialists, corrupt governments, hurricanes, and earthquakes. Diseases hit Haiti — malaria, dengue fever, cholera, typhoid, cancer, even the measles and the mumps. These illnesses leave Haitian people fighting their entire lives just to stay healthy and alive. The infant mortality rate, maternal mortality rate, and life expectancy in Haiti are grim. The infant mortality rate is ten times higher than that of the U.S. and the life expectancy is almost two decades shorter in Haiti than in most developed countries.

So, for the lady at the grocery store who asked, "Didn't they have that earthquake there a few years back? Are things any better?"

When confronted with these questions and only a moment to come up with an answer, I am truly stumped. How do we explain systemic poverty? How do we come up with pat answer solutions or explanations? And how do we get people to care enough to try to understand? Systemic poverty is alive and well in the U.S. as well. Much of the poverty here, too, is a result of systemic injustice. We may never be able to undo the wrongs and make them right, but coming alongside people who are victims or born into systemic poverty is our mandate if we are Christ followers. By definition, we are called to care and to understand and to be a part of the solution. For me it is Haiti, for you it might be somewhere in your hometown. There is no shortage of marginalized and vulnerable people in the world to whom we can be a beacon of hope.

3. In Critical Condition: A Way of Life

I have lived and worked in Haiti for almost ten years. I've learned through my own mistakes that listening is better than lecturing and that when forming models of charity, the heart of compassion must not lose touch with the brain.

Not long ago I invited a group of Haitian women I have known for years to my home for dinner. I sat across from Nadege, one of my sweet artisans who has been working with me for over seven years. She did most of the talking, though four other women sat on a couch next to her with me. So many things were on my mind and I craved their input. You can live in Haiti for a decade and not really understand what people are going through unless you take the time to sit and listen and ask difficult questions. I am so fortunate to have a handful of women in my company of artisans who have known me long enough to open up about the difficult things that they experience.

"At what point does a person get used to being hungry?" I asked. I have seen real hunger, more than I cared to in the last ten years, but I can't imagine this kind of hunger because I have never experienced it. I'm on the other end of the spectrum where I actually pay people to help me lose weight. Weight Watchers. South Beach. It's an embarrassing fact that I haven't totally come to any kind of peace about. I need them to explain true hunger to me like a seeing person explains sight to a blind man.

"I mean, is there a point where you get so used to it that you stop feeling it? How do you handle it every day?" I asked so naively.

Nadege's response illuminated how she and her children experienced hunger before she began working for Papillon.

"I can ignore it," she said in a matter-of-fact way. "Sometimes it becomes such a part of your life that you don't even notice it. You just live your life and don't pay attention to something that you can't change."

"But what about your children? Can they turn it off, too?" The very thought made me wince, not only because it pained me to think of hungry children crying for their food, but also because I remembered moments with my young family in America waiting in a restaurant for food to come. I knew the tantrums that would ensue if the waitress didn't quickly bring some breadsticks for my toddlers to snack on. Children do not hide their hunger well. Not mine, anyway. And not Haitian children either.

Nadege looked at me sadly and explained. "When they are babies they can't. They just cry and cry. We put salt under their tongues to make them thirsty so that they drink a lot of water and go to sleep."

She added that sometimes the marchanns, who sell goods in the area, will give crackers on credit. "Most of the time they won't. They know we can't pay. Sometimes a friend has a little extra to share, but not every day."

She paused, her forehead wrinkled as if she had remembered a painful moment. "We just try to rock them to sleep. They eventually cry themselves to sleep. Sleep is the great escape from hunger," Nadege said softly, still reminiscing on harder times.

Near the age of four, explained Nadege, children realize that hunger is a way of life and they settle into it. By then they know their tears won't get them what they need, and they, like their parents, learn to ignore the pangs.

We talked about hunger in the city versus the countryside.

Sonia, in her forties and one of our oldest artisans, chimed in.

"It used to be that people in the countryside had more food from their gardens. But not anymore. The hurricane that hit Gonaive in 2004 took out many of the crops that the people relied on for food. The crops still haven't grown back to how it used to be. And then, when Hurricane Matthew hit Jeremie so hard last year, several kinds of vegetables and fruit were lost. We haven't seen them since."

Nadege said, "Everything is so expensive now, too. Even bananas are expensive. We can barely afford to eat the food that is grown in our own country."

* * *

I admit I get discouraged. It seems like the challenges come exponentially to Haiti. Even though it seems like I barely make a dent, I'll keep working hard with the hope that someday meaningful change will come. And even though it may seem futile and barely noticeable that we fight so hard to keep jobs for our artisans lined up, there are two reasons I keep trying.

One: The resilient people of Haiti deserve the chance to break the cycle of crushing disappointment. They deserve to taste success. I feel that my place of privilege was given to me for the specific purpose of extending my blessings to others. An old Sunday School verse will not let me forget my place. *"From everyone who has been given much, much will be required."* Luke 12:48. There is no doubt in comparison that I have been blessed with much, and for what reason, other than to be a blessing to those who were not as fortunate?

Two: I don't look at Haiti as a country that needs to be saved. That would feel undeniably daunting and impossible. I view Haiti in terms of its individual people — my friends. Friends like Sonia, who with Nadege has taught me so much about hunger and pain. Maybe the country as a whole won't get better any time soon, but I know that Sonia's life can be radically improved by the work I do to sell her artisan goods to a global market. I have seen this mother go from being homeless and begging to leave her child at an orphanage, to becoming a dignified woman, capable of managing a department in my company. In doing so, she is supporting her children so that someday her daughter will be able to go to college. She also has a dream of finishing her own high school education. She is a middle-aged woman, digging her way out of poverty with a reading level equal to that of my Haitian son in the fourth grade, but she still has unquenchable dreams for herself.

I accept the limited sphere of my influence. I am well aware of Haiti's serious problems, but I try not to dwell on them. Rather,

I see my close Haitian friends who are struggling and naturally want to do what I can to help. By keeping my circle small, I can maintain sanity and stick with my passion. It is the only way I can live in such a vast sea of desperation and not go crazy. I focus on a chosen few whom I can be there for. And they, in turn, teach me more than I ever could have imagined about love, life, perseverance, resilience, and hope.

4. Rule of Law

*T*he text messages were blowing up on our phones. Messages were being copied and shared around Facebook. The streets are "hot." We call them *manifestations* in Haiti.

The text message spelled it out phonetically in Kreyol, the language of the people, so that everyone could understand loud and clear.

"Everyone must stay home today. Do not attempt to go to work. Do not attempt to send your child to school. Do not attempt to be out in the streets. If you do, be sure to write your name with a marker on your foot so that they will be able to identify your headless body."

The political opposition parties often gain ground through fear and intimidation. Shutting down the city gets the government's attention and the negotiations can begin. For three days, we were all grounded. The shutdown was planned ahead of time, so we had enough warning to stock up on gas and food and water in order to hunker down like we were told to.

We weren't afraid this time. We knew we weren't in danger as long as we stayed home and laid low. We carried on within the confines of our artisan facility hoping that the current political oppression would pass quickly. Several of our managers and workers couldn't get in to work that week. We encouraged them to stay home, out of harm's way until the tension in the streets subsided.

By Wednesday we were worried that we might miss a ship date and upset our clients. It is hard to keep making excuses to them.

"We are sorry, but there was no internet."

"We are sorry, but there was no gas at the pump for our cars."

"We are sorry, but there were manifestations in the streets, and we couldn't deliver your boxes to the port."

Our clients, unaware of our day-to-day struggles, can start to question our integrity as a business. We want to showcase all of what Haiti has to offer the world, but in the midst of political instability, sometimes it feels like the country is working against itself.

Rule of law is the foundation for making a country ready to take the first step out of poverty. I wrote a bit in my first book about the difficulty I found in just avoiding being threatened. Some of my friends (both Haitians and foreigners) have also endured being stolen from, broken into, robbed at gunpoint, attacked, extorted, swindled, conned, and even killed. And almost nothing was ever done about it. It requires a lot of resilience to carry on.

George led a men's Bible study in a little suburb of Port Au Prince. They found him dead and his laptop stolen. It was rumored to be someone in his Bible study, but no one knows for sure and justice was never served.

Mary and Mike were broken into and held for ransom for three days before they were finally freed unharmed. There was never any justice.

A foreign investor decided to buy land and build a factory with his fortune. He wanted to leave a legacy in the fight against poverty in Haiti. The land was disputed, didn't have a clear title, and the investor lost all his money.

A friend wanted to start a business making clothing for an online website. They went to the government offices to register the business, but not knowing where to go, he fell in with a "lawyer" who said he would help. My friend ended up losing thousands of dollars to try to get a simple business license, and eventually just quit.

I have heard story after story after story of injustice that had no recourse. People simply pack up and walk away when it gets too hard. It is hard to tolerate being taken from, tricked, and lied to when you are trying to help. Almost nobody comes to start a business in Haiti because it is the most logical place to do so. There are much more appealing and attractive countries to do business with if profits are the only thing on your mind! Most foreigners who do business in Haiti do so with social intent. They may want to make money, but they choose Haiti because they really want to help and make a difference for the poor. Their purpose is more important than profits.

But inevitably, without laws and a path to find justice when wrong befalls you, it is nearly impossible to keep up the will to stay. Corruption is an issue that missionaries and aid organizations just can't deal with. Justice and laws must be created and upheld by the government and by the Haitian people through voting and determination. Someone once told me that Haiti runs "exactly as it is intended to run." Perhaps those in power profit from the way it is. The chaos and corruption allow for those in control to get richer and benefit from the way things are. Maybe poverty and corruption and lawlessness serve them well? The poor people are a magnet for foreign aid workers, and the government can rely on outsiders to do the job they were intended to do. Haiti is also notorious for being part of the massive highway for the drug trade. Who benefits from the steady stream of cocaine? And why would they want it to dry up?

Some days it seems impossible to function as a normal business. My ideals feel foolish and unattainable. I certainly won't change Haiti. That is for Haitians to do. But I can as a fellow human being help those around me in the way that I am gifted. Not because of pity, but because they are indeed just like me in every way. Just as capable. Given the same opportunity, many of them would have done so much more than I ever have. They deserve a chance.

5. An Apology for Systemic Poverty

*B*lack Lives Matter. It is a mantra that will go down in history. Blame is placed on both sides, then dodged and misplaced. The truth is that we don't all start with the same hand of cards. There is no arguing that men have more advantages than women in the workforce. There is no conscious person who wouldn't admit that historical problems have resulted in systemic stereotyping and racism. My Haitian son Jackson is treated differently than my white son Zebedee. They have both had the same platform of opportunity, but the subtle expectations by teachers, shop owners, and friends are clear as day. People don't expect the same things out of them. How can my ten-year-old Haitian son not let those expectations define him to some degree? The unintended curses of the world hang over his head and give him much more to fight against.

Marginalized voices need to be heard. People from hard places need to be treated with care. We who are born into affluence and opportunity can never know the level of difficulty others face to get to same place where we stand, unaware of our head start. They run through quicksand while we run on firm gravel. There is nothing fair about this race. We might not know how to fix it, but we would do well to at least acknowledge it and respect the struggle.

I can't do anything to change history and very little to change systems. But I can do something for the person in front of me. I have been given much and much is and should be required of me.

SECTION 2

Go Into All the World:
The Heart of Christian Missions

Mark 16:15
"Go into all the world and preach
the good news to all creation."

*M*issional Christianity was a proclamation of restoration of relationship between God and humans. The signs that accompanied the proclamation of good news included *physical* healing, feeding people, and other physical restoration. If God cared only about heaven, why would He care about our temporal bodies? Why was Jesus moved to give lunch to 5,000 hungry people, heal sickness, and tell his followers to care for the poor if he didn't care about the plight of the suffering on earth today? It is the duty of Christ followers to not only preach the restoration of relationship to God but also to be a part of the healing of the world today. *Both are the gospel!*

1. Missionary Life: Cultural Considerations

A team of missionaries sit on the airplane. Their bright orange shirts populate the seats making it look more like a sporting event than a commercial airliner. The shirts say "Hope for Haiti" in bold letters and on the back is a scripture verse in bold serif font.

I sit on the plane minding my own business, and the lady next to me in a khaki skirt, sandals, and the orange T-shirt leans over and smiles cheerfully. Her teeth are perfect and her hair, showing just a tiny bit of grey, is pulled neatly in a ponytail.

"What are you going to do in Haiti?" she asks me with an inflected upswing at the end of the sentence. She is full of excitement.

Not wanting to get too much into it, and wanting to get some work done, I tell her I work in manufacturing in Haiti. It's a boring answer that usually ends the conversation.

It doesn't this time. She asks more questions, and I end up telling my story about wanting to help keep families intact by providing jobs for parents.

She listens like she has no idea what I'm talking about.

I pause, and she just stares at the seat in front of her. I break the silence by asking her the question I assume she is dying to answer.

"And what about you? What are you all doing this week?"

"We're doing evangelism. We're going out to the country-side to our sister church and working with the pastor there to tell the Haitians about Jesus."

I smile politely and say, "Well, that's great! I hope you have a great week."

I get off the plane a few hours later where my driver picks me up. On the way home, we are caught up in traffic and find ourselves in a sea of tap-taps, the Haitian form of public trans-portation. Brightly painted trucks are modified with bench seats and roofs and can transport up to twenty people in the truck bed. The vehicles are painted bright colors and often have por-traits of famous people. The one next to us says "Jesus is King" with a crude painting of Jesus on a cross. The one behind us says in bright yellow letters "Glory to God" with angels painted on each side of the tap tap. The one just two cars ahead proclaims "Christ is Capable" with artwork to match.

I think about the lady coming to tell Haitians about Jesus. We pass by a church on the corner packed to the brim and over-flowing with Wednesday night services characterized by fervent prayer and worship. Haitian men race to the door dressed to the hilt in suits and ties, with big Bibles tucked under their arms.

Haitians know about Jesus.

It is an anomaly to meet a Haitian person who doesn't esteem being a Christian. Being a pastor is a well-respected position. It is a place of power and authority.

So, what then is the disconnect? Why are missionaries coming to talk about Jesus when more Haitians per capita claim to be Christian than Americans do? Why does Haiti appear to outsiders to be an unreached people in need of missionaries when they are so clearly open to and accepting of the Christian gospel and faith? Over the years I have made a couple of observations that may explain why planeloads of missionaries keep coming in droves to preach the gospel.

2. Money and Power

*H*aiti is poor. Decades ago when the bravest of missionaries decided to leave the comforts of their homelands and travel to Haiti to spread the Christian gospel, they quickly realized that they had more to offer than simply the Biblical narrative. Because of the imbalance of resources, the white missionaries quickly became a financial resource instead of just the catalyst for converts. It is hard to keep the true Christian conversion experience authentic when it is accompanied by financial benefit or material resources. Perhaps that is why the Biblical mandate to the first disciples was to venture out with nothing but the clothes on their backs and to live at the mercy of hospitality rather than what they might make along the way. All they had to give was to be the good news of a loving God wanting a relationship with the human beings He had created. While this book is about poverty alleviation and I fully believe in the gospel as described above, it is a surprisingly tricky and delicate matter to do both evangelism and charity in tandem *for long periods of time.*

As we've seen throughout history, from the time of Constantine through the Middle Ages and even the colonization of America, the gospel mixed with undo profiting results in a distortion of that gospel. Christianity quickly becomes something very different in nature when mixed with economics, politics, and power. Jesus loved the poor and he also didn't hesitate to call his followers to a life of poverty — perhaps, among other reasons, to avert this very problem of distortion and corruption. People are smart. The poor quickly figure out how to acquire the goods coming in with the missionaries. Conversions, salvations, and affirmations are easily obtained when the rewards are much-needed donations to provide for their families. And this overwhelming response makes the missionary feel successful and needed. It is a win-win on the emotional and economic front.

The realization that missionaries like to work with the "local church" has Haitian men lining up to be pastors. To become one creates a place of power and position. Pastors are held in high esteem as they become the gate keeper to much-needed resources. Everyone becomes a Christian when bags of rice are involved. Any smart local will go to the missionary meeting and raise their hands to accept Christ. The cycle of success continues as long as donations for the poor accompany the missions' trips. The authenticity of it all, however, is in question for me.

But the nice smiley lady on the plane doesn't know all of this and she is just excited. The faith that she holds so dearly will finally find ears with the Haitians she is going *to serve*. They may have heard it a hundred times before, but they will act like it is the first time ever when she shares it. They will call her "sister" and she will feel a part of the larger community of Christians, and so will the team coming to evangelize next week, and the next, and the next. Over and over.

It is the way of life. It is how pastors make a living. It is a failsafe mission trip. Everyone leaves happy and fulfilled. I wonder how it is perceived, however, from the heavenlies when so much money is spent to fly in and convert already converted poor people. I want to reserve judgement, but something tells me our integrity as people of faith might be in question.

The power dynamics create a more complicated and sinister back story. A pastor does not become a pastor based on his character and commitment to the teachings of Christ or his education necessarily in Biblical principles and scripture. His ability to preach with conviction, using words he has never really been trained in but can spew out eloquently in theatrical rants, gets him the job. He is an entertainer. His church grows because he speaks enough English to attract the missionaries to return repeatedly, and because he has learned the art of public speaking.

But he may not be a man after God's own heart. He keeps his hair short, makes women wear dresses, and keeps the poorly dressed street kids outside the church where they belong. He speaks sharply about a woman's role and about gambling and tattoos and alcohol. He has learned well from the American church of the 1950's who first brought their legacy of conservatism and a strict moral code. But he has perhaps never been taught about and doesn't know a loving Father. His message is judgment and hell and repentance. He was never introduced to the tender heart of God.

And perhaps, behind the eloquent rants, he is trying, like the rest of his neighbors, just to meet his daily needs. In his role as pastor, he is the gatekeeper of the donations. Greed has been known to get the upper hand and sets in until he justifies why he takes his share of the money and builds himself a nice house instead of spreading it equally with his congregation who are struggling to eat every day. His success only gives him more clout.

"If you follow God, success will come to you as well." Prosperity gospel is a convenient apologetic for his wealth. And it works, too!

The congregation's desperate need for help compels them to believe him. He takes it a step further. If you give to the church — just $15 a week — he will personally pray over your money and you will be blessed. Give $30 and God Almighty will grant you a visa to the promised land: the United States of America. (I'm not making this stuff up!)

His congregation believes him. They are desperate for hope. The richer he gets, the more his prophecy of "the blessings" of following God ring true. He is now the wealthiest person in his village. Women make themselves available to him. He is the king of his domain.

While this story is not a description of every pastor and church by any means, in my experience it was hard to find a pastor during my time in Haiti who was not influenced by the power and resources that he was privy to. It was hard to find one who resembled the Jesus I knew who protected prostitutes and let the dirty little kids come to him. Truth be told, I never encountered a pastor in Haiti like that.

To many, Christianity has become the pathway to prosperity and power rather than the discovery of a God who loves and desires personal intimacy and connection. I have often thought that the only way to truly and absolutely know whether faith and conversion and evangelism are authentic is to arrive with nothing, like the early believers, and to give nothing but the love of God. To live as they live and have nothing that puts us in a power position over them.

But that is nearly impossible.

Even if we stripped ourselves bare, we would still have an upper hand, a safety net, experience, or resources that they would want.

Is it hopeless then? Do true conversions exist that are not overshadowed by handouts and aid? How do we meet the needs of people who are poor and need help as much as they need to hear about our heavenly Father? So many questions like these have haunted me during my years in Haiti. I would argue that this is not unique to Haiti and is perhaps a worldwide phenomenon for Western missions to the developing world. How can we do it better?

I wonder if perhaps true gospel must come from within Haiti's own ranks. I long to see a Christianity embodied by humility, grace, love, and kindness present in Haiti. So far, I have found it to be incredibly rare. Evangelism is needed. There is no doubt in my mind that many converts have never really understood the core message of the gospel. Grace. Love. Forgiveness. But I am not so sure that the woman on the plane next to me is the one to present the authentic gospel. I hope for a day when I see Haitian locals, empowered by the love of their Jesus, forsake the rules and regulations of the law of the church and become a force of LOVE in this country. That is what Haiti truly needs: the endless and boundless love of God made transparent to the hearts of the people. The love that says that street kids, and prostitutes, and even sneaky pastors are loved and welcomed 100% by God unconditionally.

3. Another Way

*T*he purpose of missions has traditionally been defined as evangelism and charity. I wholeheartedly support both approaches but am compelled to wonder how we can do it better after seeing the fallout of rampant charity destroying industry, dignity, faith, and economic growth in the countries and people groups that we are trying to help. We continue to put bandages and antiseptic on gaping wounds without thinking about how we could be part of a permanent solution. It takes so much more time and work and feels way less emotionally satisfying to dig in and do long hard work than the spiritual high we gain from a week-long mission trip. In some ways, true missions don't feel spiritual at all.

Mission work, for me, is not just about evangelism. My faith compels me to use my brain and do something to help with a more permanent solution, though it might not feel as spiritual. I find the model of teaching people to fish rather than giving them fish to be tried and true wisdom. I have seen that trying to feed a nation of people is not only futile and never-ending, but does nothing to solve the problem of poverty over the long run. Moving away from traditional hand-out models of charity doesn't feel as good, but we must believe that we are gifted to use our minds to come up with real solutions instead of temporary patches that give us all the feels yet offer no real long-term hope.

Missionary work comes in so many different forms. Discipleship, life skills training, evangelism, and education are all part of helping the poor. But we have to start asking the tough questions. How do we not contaminate or distort the gospel in the process? It takes humility and hard work to reevaluate missions. A behind-the-scenes look at many missions' models can all too often reveal a facade that keeps money flowing in and checks a box for those who need to *feel* useful and activate their faith.

In my experience, the path to understanding lies in honest conversations with long-term missionaries and honest locals *who don't need anything from you*. Most of them know the truth, and most of them are tired of being unheard. They can seem cynical, jaded, or hostile toward short-term missionaries, and oftentimes quite rightly so. Years of seeing futile attempts to help with reckless aid and handouts coupled with the misuse of scarce and needed resources have left them scarred, but they have a wealth of experience and knowledge that we would be wise to tap into if we are to honestly evaluate our mission models. Are we truly furthering the kingdom of God by putting on matching T-shirts and spending thousands of dollars traveling for a week to preach the gospel to people who have heard it twice as many times as there are weeks in the year?

Perhaps that mission week is much more about us. Maybe the radical change that occurs in us as we are forced to face poverty and dig deeper with God for answers is what short-term missions is really about. I don't think there is anything wrong with that and celebrate self-reflection and personal growth as its own end goal, *as long as it does no harm*. But integrity and honesty about this process would be refreshing to me and to many who have lived for any length of time as a long-term missionary in a poverty culture.

SECTION 3

I Will Not Leave You as Orphans: Why the Poverty Orphan?

Isaiah 1:17
"Learn to do good; seek justice, correct oppression;
bring justice to the fatherless, plead the widow's cause."

*L*ife is full of contradictions and this section will seem at first to contradict so much of what I have laid out so far. I am willing to risk that. It is important for me to paint a clear picture of the real and urgent needs that Haitians face. It is important for the reader to understand the world that the poor are born into and what makes a poverty orphan such a common occurrence in a place like Haiti and the rest of the developing world.

I want to acknowledge and embrace the grey areas of helping the poor. It is not ALL charity, ALL evangelism, or ALL job creation. For a situation like Haiti, it is often (carefully) both or all three at the same time. My hope is that we continue a trajectory that leads to the physical, mental, and spiritual restoration of people's lives. But we are not there yet. And times of crisis do call for immediate intervention.

Before I go any further, I have to describe some of the situations I have encountered that brought me to a place of desperately wanting to find real solutions for systemic poverty. The stories outlined below will hopefully do just that.

1. Ransom

*J*osue knocked on my gate. I didn't really like Josue. He was the neighborhood con artist, had a weird-shaped head, and usually had a creepy look on his face. He spoke enough English to be able to lie his way into a handout from most of the missionaries in the neighborhood before they figured him out, but he never really ever went away, always roaming the streets looking for fresh missionaries to tell tall tales to.

I cracked open the gate and rolled my eyes. "What do you want? I told you I don't want you coming over any more." I had banned him from the property after he stole a camera and conned me out of a substantial amount of money.

I could see he had something to tell me he thought was important, but I was so tired of his stories, I almost shut the gate on his nose that was trying to poke in through the crack.

"Shelley please, listen. My friend needs some help. She has a baby that has been taken away from her."

I stopped the gate short of his nose and paused. He had hit a nerve. Everyone knew I was a sucker for babies and mamas in need. I had just begun my small start-up business employing women who were struggling to take care of their children.

"They won't let her have her baby," he pleaded.

"What do you mean they won't let her have her baby?" I retorted skeptically.

"She just had her baby yesterday morning at the hospital down the street. She doesn't have any money to pay the bill, so they are holding the baby. They won't let the baby leave until she pays. And Shelley … she is bleeding a lot."

"Who is bleeding?" I shot back.

"The mother, my friend is bleeding. She needs help."

"Where exactly is she?" I could feel myself taking the bait.

"Around the corner," he motioned. "Just down by the church on the corner."

It was about a half mile away at most.

My interest had been piqued.

I didn't trust Josue, but if what he was saying was true, I didn't want a mother to die because of his character flaws and general lack of decency.

I agreed to accompany him to the hospital to see what the deal was. We left on foot as I knew it was close enough, and I always liked to walk any chance I had to get out of my four walls and barbed wire.

No more than six blocks from my house we came to a green and white painted gate, the colors for medical clinics and hospitals. I had never noticed the building before. It was a seemingly normal one-story house on the main road in a residential area that had simply been painted and turned into a maternity clinic.

I followed Josue through the gate and across the concrete courtyard. He led me past the iron window bars painted white. The door to the house was flung wide open, begging for a slight breeze in the Haitian heat.

We entered the building. In the first room on the right, a woman in an otherwise empty room dressed in a nurse's uniform slumped over her desk taking a nap. It didn't look like much was going on today.

We continued past another bedroom with an empty bed in it and then down a hallway, where we went straight into an open-doored room.

As I followed Josue, I was stunned by what I saw.

There were two single beds in the room. On one was a small bundle wrapped in a blanket and placed in the center. The infant was sleeping. On the other bed, a woman with wild hair and desperate eyes raised her head and looked up at me.

She had a white hospital gown on but was otherwise naked. Her hair was a mess and standing on end. She was lying down on a plastic mattress with no sheets or pillow. Her face looked tired and distressed. My eyes traced her figure from her face down her body and stopped midway in horror. She was lying in a pool of blood that had collected around her body in the center of the plastic green mattress. The indentation of her body had not created enough space for the blood, and it dripped steadily on the floor next to her. Blood was collecting under her bed at an alarming rate.

"Oh my gosh!" My hands went to my mouth. "What's going on here?" I was nearly shouting.

The baby jerked its tiny hands with a startled reflex. My eyes welled up with tears.

"She just had a baby." Josue looked at me kind of funny.

"But why is there blood everywhere? Where is the nurse?" I was still shocked by the sight in front of me.

I must have made enough noise to wake up the sleeping nurse from the first room because she came sauntering in just then. The blood and my hysteria didn't faze her.

"What's going on here?" I repeated in broken Kreyol. "Why isn't this woman getting care?"

"She doesn't have money," the nurse sighed sleepily.

The mother rested her head again and started sobbing. "They won't let me leave with my baby until I can pay," she said.

Pay for what? I thought to myself.

She had been there for thirty-six hours. In a gown. No pads. Bleeding.

"We need to sew her, too." The nurse motioned to the blood. "She tore pretty badly."

"Well, why don't you sew her then?" I shot back in horror.

"Pa gen lajan." She clapped her hands together in a cultural sign of resignation. No money.

I was baffled. "She has no money, so you won't sew her?"

"No, she has no money to buy the thread and needles."

The hospital did not have thread and needles.

"Well, how much does it cost?" I asked.

"About 300 gourdes at the pharmacy up the street." She pointed in the direction of a pharmacy I knew to be just around the corner.

I had brought money with me, assuming the situation might require it. I turned to Josue who had been standing silent.

"Can you go buy the needle and thread if I give you the money?" I asked politely because I had all but forgiven him by this point. He had brought me to the right place. "I only have U.S. dollars. Here is $10. Bring back the change."

Josue nodded and jogged off toward the pharmacy just up the street.

The needle and thread would amount to about $7.50. The nurse, realizing that someone with money was around who could probably foot the bill for the lady, brought me an invoice for services. Fifty-five dollars was owed the hospital for delivering the baby. She had been held hostage, possibly left to bleed to death, for lack of $62.50.

I paid the bill, and after an unhurried receipt was written, the nurse motioned for the mother to get up from the bed and follow her. The woman got up, still dripping blood, and followed the nurse down the hallway. At the end, a room opened to the right. A chair with stirrups was the only piece of furniture. The nurse motioned for the patient to sit down and put her feet up.

I worried about the baby and went back to check. Still sleeping.

By the time I got back to the medical room, the mother's legs were spread open. No privacy and her wounds were in full view. The area was swollen and looked painful. I remembered back to how that felt from my own childbirth experiences. This woman had been without care for quite some time.

As we waited for delivery of the thread and needles, the nurse picked at her fingernails, while the mother closed her eyes, wincing in pain. The clock in the office across the hall kept ticking the incorrect time, until finally we heard the hospital gate open and slam shut.

Josue appeared, and we were now ready for the prodedure —without anesthesia, of course. That was too expensive, and anyway the hospital had run out. The nurse stepped into the hallway and made a phone call. Then she wiped down the wincing mother with a brown iodine solution and prepped for the procedure. A few minutes later, an older woman entered and sat down to begin the sewing. She had a gruff voice and showed no signs of compassion as her needle pierced the tender genital area. The mother winced and wailed.

I could not believe what I was seeing. I couldn't fully digest the emotional and physical toll this poor woman had endured. Then it occurred to me that no one was there with her. Just Josue and me. Where was the father? I wondered. Where was her mother?

I could hardly bear it, so I walked down the hallway, in tears, and did not turn back until the stitches had all been put in place.

Suddenly the doctor, if that is what she was, stood up and motioned to me, "All done. She can go."

At that point, the nurse entered the room with the baby. The infant was placed in the mother's arms and we were shown the door.

"You can go now," the nurse said. I looked at Josue. "Just like that? She's walking out of the hospital now in this condition?" And in her gown?

The mother was limping, hobbled by the procedure and weight of her baby. Each step looked extremely painful.

Josue grabbed the baby to help his friend.

"How is she getting home?" I asked.

The nurse motioned toward the door. "Tap-tap just down the street."

Tap-taps and their metal bench seats are indeed a common way to travel in Port au Prince, but for a bruised and battered new mother and her baby?

"Wait right there." I motioned for her to stay put. "I'm going to get my car."

I sprinted the six blocks home and darted inside just long enough to tell the workers helping me with laundry that I would be right back and to watch my kids for a few minutes more. I grabbed the keys and sped away in my beat-up silver Toyota 4Runner.

At the hospital, Josue and I helped the woman and her baby into the back seat of my car. She cried out in pain as she tried to find a comfortable position. She explained that sitting was impossible. She would need to lie down. She laid across the back seats and tried to tolerate the pain for the short bumpy ride home.

Josue got in the front seat with the baby. There are no enforced car seat laws in Haiti, and infants and small children are usually held by adult passengers.

We drove about a mile up the street to the Delmas 60 slum area of Port Au Prince. Josue guided me to a side road that took us through an alley and up to a little one-room hut with a single tree next to it.

"This is where she lives," Josue said.

We pulled close and parked.

The concrete building was about ten by ten feet square. Lace curtains that adorned the doorway fluttered in the breeze. A face peeked out. It was a neighbor. She clapped her hands and ushered the mother inside. I followed.

A double bed, a shelf for dishes, a pile of clothes in a basket in one corner, and a small, stained place for cooking was all that was in the house.

The mother laid the baby down in the center of the bed and crawled in close to her, exhausted.

"Congratulations," I said. Trying to be encouraging. "You have a baby girl."

The woman returned my smile. "Mesi anpil," she whispered, thanking me for what I did for her.

"No problem," I whispered back, as I bent over to get a closer look at the child. "My first baby was a girl, too. What will you name her?" I asked.

She looked up at me and shrugged. "I don't know yet."

Her head relaxed into a pillow and I felt like it was time for me to go. As Josue and I began to leave she lifted her head and said, "Wait. What is your name?"

"Me? My name is Shelley." I smiled.

She put her head down again, then said, "My daughter will be named Shelley, too."

Josue smiled at me as I thanked the woman for the honor.

Once we were in the car, Josue said, "Thank you for helping her. You didn't have to do that."

"Yes, I did, Josue. Yes, I did."

Somewhere out there a baby has turned into a little girl who bears my name. I never saw the mother or child again. But I will always remember that day. I was blessed to be in the right place at the right time. It cost me $62.50 so that a baby would have a mother and the mother could go home with her newborn. These moments became the foundation for my philosophy on orphan care. What I began to realize was that every child in need was the product of a mother or father in a desperate situation. The parents were the ones who needed help to prevent their children from ever becoming orphans.

Anyone with a heart would have done the same in that situation. But I was chosen by divine intervention with the blessing of a knock on the gate by my now-favorite neighborhood con artist.

Josue continues to this day to roam the streets and tell his stories. I don't pay him much attention anymore, but I always remember the day he came to me and helped save baby Shelley and her mother. This was the beginning of my life calling to orphan prevention.

2. Night at the Maternity Center

The experiences that led me to understand how poverty was the enemy to orphan prevention were unrelenting. Once, at about 5 p.m., I was finishing up a nice day at the artisan house, working with several ladies on beading, when Rodney, one of our "street boys," approached me and said his mom was sick… again…and would I come to their tent. They lived in one of the larger tent cities in our area, a community of about five thousand people.

My curiosity for how people managed to live in these tent communities day after day had piqued my interest enough that I had camped with them for almost a week and gotten to know Rodney's family of seven children in one small tent pretty well. The conditions proved to be much harder than I expected, and it gave me more respect for what the poor in these situations must endure just to get through the day. Rose, Rodney's mom, also worked as a jewelry artisan alongside me and she had quickly become one of my favorite artisans. How she came to work smelling good and with crisp, clean clothes on every day despite living in those conditions is still a mystery to me. Rose was a slender woman with a wide jaw and either a big smile or a menacing scowl depending on what kind of mood she was in. She had ongoing health issues, including chronic migraines, so I was used to hearing that she was sick. Still, I wanted to find out what was going on.

That rainy afternoon, I made the trek with Rodney into their tent city to check in on her, but she was nowhere to be found. After inquiring with the neighbors, I learned that at some point during the day she had passed out and been allegedly taken to a hospital nearby. Her husband, too, had just come home from work and was also worried about what had happened to her and wondering where she was.

In the maze of Haiti's tent cities and broken-down buildings, it's not always easy to locate people, or buildings even, but we decided to try to find her and figured the hospital was the best place to start. The earthquake had left the city a bit of a labyrinth that was slow to be repaired. At the time, even the hospitals were operating out of tents. After striking out twice with wrong hospitals, we found a third option that we were pretty sure was the only other place they could have taken her. The tent hospital operated like a fortress. Resources being scarce, they turned people away daily and were hesitant to let anyone in. We argued with the guards for fifteen minutes about gaining admittance to the grounds to look for Rose, and eventually they were able to be coerced when they realized our determination to find our friend.

The "hospital" itself was a maze of interconnected tunnels of tents, like a humongous living room of play fortresses from when I was five years old — only much more menacing. We walked from tent to tent in the pouring evening rain trying to find Rose. Time and again we were told that nobody by her name had been admitted. I have found in Haiti and in life that "No" is often the easy answer when it is inconvenient to find a real answer. Thus, I'm not one who easily takes "No" for an answer.

We held out hope that she was in that hospital because quite frankly, we were out of places they could have taken her. Finally, we opened a tent flap to peer inside and saw a crazy mess of hair sticking out from behind a partial wall for privacy. On closer look I saw Rose's familiar face, pale and grim now with a locked broad jaw. Something was seriously wrong. Rose was being hooked up to a bag of IV fluids. Upon further conversation with the doctor on call, we learned that they suspected an ectopic pregnancy.

Rose was shocked and dismayed by the positive pregnancy test.

Her body stiffened with renewed tension. She was not a wilting violet. As sick as she felt, this mother of seven had spunk that never quit, and she promptly began yelling at the nurses in angry denial. They attempted to calm her down, saying she needed to rest and save her strength.

Giving birth to her last baby via C-section just a year ago, Rose had almost lost her life and vowed she would never risk another pregnancy, so she had been taking her birth control religiously. Hot tears of fear and frustration hit the bed that Rose lay on. She was in pain, anemic, and not strong enough to carry a baby. Worse, she might not be strong enough to go through another surgery, but that was appearing to be her only recourse for staying alive.

Even if Rose was approved to go through the emergency surgery in her weakened state, the hospital didn't have the equipment it needed or the surgeons to perform it. Yet without the surgery, and quickly, she would probably die. Seven children would lose their mother.

Having no other alternative and caving in to the reality of the situation, Rose agreed to seek treatment if we could find a hospital that could help. The thought of her babies growing up without a mother compelled her. The nearest hospital known to be capable of providing the surgery she needed was near Cite Soleil, one of the most dangerous areas in Haiti, known for its regular gang violence and extreme poverty. It was nearing nightfall, the worst time to brave that area. But we knew it couldn't wait until morning. It was never a question in our minds whether Rose's life was worth the risk. We quickly turned my beaten up 4Runner into a makeshift ambulance and in the pouring rain and flooded streets headed into Cite Soleil to the maternity hospital as darkness rapidly approached.

The maternity hospital was nothing I could have prepared myself for. Even from outside, the cries of pain were ominous and heart wrenching. A guard stood at the entrance to be sure that only women in labor entered the building. There simply wasn't enough room for visitors to accompany anyone. So many of the alternate maternity centers had been damaged in the earthquake and there weren't enough centers to accommodate any additional medical needs. In spite of their strict rules about visitors, they allowed me to enter with Rose because of the status that my skin color offered me. Most "white" people were perceived to be relief workers bringing aid in some form or another and so access to hospitals was easier to negotiate. Most of the women inside were by themselves, many of them crying in the dark hospital that was running on a generator that allowed only a few lights in the operating and administrative rooms. With no family or friends for comfort, every woman looked so very alone in a time of great need for comfort. It was hard to watch.

It only got worse as I entered the labor and delivery room. There were no fewer than fifty women in labor, on the floor, in the hallways, screaming, bleeding, all by themselves. Five valiant doctors were running around doing their best to handle birth after birth, but it was obvious they had become numb to the pain around them. I looked over at a woman on a dirty plastic-covered piece of cardboard for a bed. She was bleeding. This is hell, I thought.

I had the privilege of standing beside Rose and massaging her feet and stroking her head and explaining what an ectopic pregnancy was and letting her know exactly what to expect. So many of the other women in the large open rooms had no idea what was happening to their bodies, and no one was there to give them an ounce of information or comfort. These women had almost certainly never been taught basic anatomy or had a childbirth class, either of which would ease their anxiety and fear of the unknown.

Rose cried as it settled in on her that the time for surgery was looming. She, too, was horrified by the dismal conditions of the hospital. She looked at me and said, "Shelley, Map mouri." Shelley, I'm going to die.

"You can do this, Rose," I said. "You can do this for your children and your family. You're going to be okay."

Most of the girls there seemed to either be from Cite Soleil itself or had come in from the countryside to give birth in the only known hospital still standing after the earthquake. A fifteen-year-old girl, terrified and giving birth to her first child on a floor in an overcrowded hospital, was a reminder of the plight of women all over the world. Women feel the consequences of poverty acutely. It seems that women bear the brunt of so much more than men do.

My attention turned to Rose. She was on the pre-op exam table, being prepped for surgery by the overly occupied doctors. I shuddered to think where she would have been in line if I hadn't come in with her and wondered if she would have made it through the night. Right before she went into surgery I asked the doctors if they could tie her tubes. It was something Rose and I had discussed on the way over. The doctors argued with me. She is too young, they said.

Rose was thirty-five and had seven children.

"She doesn't need any more kids," I said. "Right, Rose?" I looked at her and she nodded and agreed fervently. The doctor designated to her surgery shrugged his shoulders and lazily agreed to tie her tubes.

Rose wrinkled her nose and lifted her arm and began to wag her finger at the doctor, her legs still in the examination stirrups.

"If Shelley wasn't here, you wouldn't have done that for me," she scolded him. She looked at me and nodded her head with a punctuation. To this day she credits me for saving her life and thanks me for making them tie her tubes.

Rose made it okay. She was whisked away to surgery that night, largely because of my presence. The perception of wealth and power goes a long way in a country like Haiti and by being with her that night, I brought attention to her that she would not have received otherwise. It is not lost on me the privilege that we who were born in America walk around with. We are perceived a certain way whether we like it or not.

On my way out of the hospital that night, after I knew Rose had made it safely through surgery, a lady in labor grabbed my arm and spoke to me in Creole. She thought I might be able to help her too. She had been in labor for four days now, her baby was dead in her womb, and no doctor had time to help her.

I looked around at the needs in that place and felt overwhelmed. I motioned to the administrative staff to come take a look at her, but I needed to get home as my own children were waiting for me. I knew I wouldn't be able to see it through with her. The doctors there couldn't help her because of the shortage of resources, and me being only one person had to realize, neither could I. It wasn't the first or the last time I turned away a mother in need. And the guilt from it remains.

3. Restaveks: The Hidden Orphan

*L*ife in Haiti is hard. Basic household chores require much more manual labor than we are accustomed to in more developed countries. Handwashing clothes, preparing food from scratch, drawing and carrying water for drinking and bathing all require more time than many women can manage on their own. When a lower to middle class Haitian family needs "house help" but can't afford a maid, it is not unusual for them to find an impoverished family or relative out in the countryside and offer to have one of their children come live with them. Typically, the offer is that the child will go to school and be cared for in exchange for helping with domestic duties. These children are called *restaveks*, derived from the French words meaning to "stay with." The reality of what happens with restavek children is not usually so pleasant. The arrangement leaves the child servant in a vulnerable and precarious situation. My artisans tell me that most children who are restaveks are mistreated — physically, mentally, and often sexually. The notoriously harsh treatment of restavek children is what has led them to be known as "child slaves" and this portrayal has left a stain on the humanitarian reputation of Haiti.

I sat on my couch with several of my artisans, some of whom had been raised as restaveks themselves, and asked them about their experiences.

Clotilde's parents died when she was a baby. Reluctantly, a distant aunt took Clotilde in with the understanding that she was to be raised as a restavek. Her aunt's two daughters also lived in Clotilde's new home, but even though they were the same age as her, it was made clear that she would not be treated like they were. Clotilde got up at 4 a.m. every morning to start making the family breakfast. After breakfast, she helped her aunt get her cousins ready for school. While they were at school, she would begin washing the clothes for the day, make endless trips to draw water, and start preparations for dinner — something that would take several hours each day. At dinner time, when she had finished making the food, she was not allowed to eat with the family, but instead was told to wait for the leftovers.

Clotilde's aunt, who was home with her for much of the day, had a small television in the two-room house. Her aunt would spend her days on the bed watching television and barking orders at Clotilde. Clotilde was to do everything that she was ordered to do or be beaten.

Clotilde sat on the couch of my house and showed me the scars on her wrists from the handwashing she did until her wrists were raw and bloody. Other scars on her body were the result of the beatings with an electrical wire if she did not get her chores done in time.

Clotilde, still sitting across from me, finished her story and we sat in silence for a second.

"Clotilde?" I asked gently.

"How do you feel now about yourself? Does it make you sad that you were treated this way?" It was perhaps the first time in her life she had been asked a self-reflective question.

"I don't really feel like I matter at all," she replied after a second of thought.

How could she feel like she mattered? How can someone endure that kind of treatment? My head still spins to imagine how she copes. How does she find joy and value?

My evangelical upbringing wondered how she felt like God fit into her story. I asked her if she was ever mad at God or her aunt.

"I'm not mad at my aunt," she replied. "She was the only mother I ever had."

I shook my head in disbelief. This was not the response I anticipated. I would be so angry if it were me. I was angry *for* her.

I asked her again about God. Did she ever wonder where He was in it all?

The other ladies who were sitting with us silently on my couch in the living room suddenly chimed in. "Yes," they all murmured. "Sometimes we ask God why we were even born. Why did He bring us into this misery?"

I asked if they were *mad* at God because they were poor and hungry and abused as children.

"No," they shook their heads. "How can we be mad at God? It is He that gives us our bodies and our breaths every day. Without Him, we are nothing."

Their response floored me.

I asked if they felt like God loved them. Again, I was so curious as to how they made sense of it all. But immediately I wondered how *could* they know His love? How could Clotilde possibly know the love of God after all she had endured?

Her eyes rose to meet mine. "Yes. Yes, I know that God loves me. I never doubt that He does." She didn't elaborate any further. I sat speechless. I wondered then and still ponder on this. How many times does God make himself known and present to the poor? I think of the darkest times in my life and how somehow I knew He was there. But still I wondered how people who are born into such extreme injustice retain that simple faith. (And how much deeper that faith seems to be.) How much I had to learn from these women. Our God is present in suffering. Clotilde knew He loved her.

Her faith astounds me. It teaches me every day that people can survive. They can even thrive. Despite it all. If only my own attitude in life were half as pure, I thought to myself. I love the tender moments when I learn so much from the artisans I work with. It is the paradigm shift of my life. This idea that the poor have so much more to offer me than I could ever give. So many people come to "teach" in Haiti. We usually barge into their worlds sitting firmly in the seat of our power position. We are the ones with the education, the money, the resources, the opportunity, and we expect that they have much more to gain from us. What I have learned over the years is that allowing yourself to be taught and allowing your life to be changed by them is where the real treasure and wealth lies. Clotilde's simple faith and honesty has a profoundness to it that I found remarkable and life-impacting.

Clotilde has been working for Papillon for six years now. She has a sweet nine-year-old daughter who runs up and throws her arms around me in greeting every time I visit them at their home. Magdala is tough like her mother. It blesses me to know that her daughter can be raised with a mother who loves her and can provide for her to go to school. Her job has given her daughter the opportunity that she never had.

Thousands of children in Haiti are living as restaveks. Mothers and fathers with no way to care for their children take desperate measures with the hope that another family will be able to give their children what they could not. Sadly, the vulnerable children often find themselves in a worse situation than the parents could ever have imagined. They are the orphans that you don't find in orphanages.

Many larger NGO's and aid organizations are working to stop the system of restaveks. Progress is being made on this front, but so much still needs to be done. Poverty created the need for the restavek, and until the harsh conditions of poverty are relieved, I suspect that vulnerable children will continue to be used in this way.

It is a sticky job to try to help restaveks themselves. Host families aren't going to part with them easily, and birth parents are hard to locate. Several good organizations are working with families who host restaveks to negotiate the opportunity for the children to at least attend school. The government is also clamping down on abuse. But the work is slow, and poverty's grip on a culture is not easy to break.

Opportunity for education is often a main motivator as to why parents place their children as restaveks and also into orphanages. If more missions and NGO's focused on good, quality schools, the numbers of children being placed in these highly vulnerable places would decrease.

4. The Poverty Orphan

*W*hen I attended a small Christian liberal arts college in the Pacific Northwest, students were encouraged to put in volunteer hours each semester. A program at the local hospital asked for volunteers to hold premature babies in its neonatal intensive care unit (NICU). I signed up immediately and was disappointed to learn that the waiting list for students was more than a year long. I should not have been surprised. People are drawn to hands-on care. It gives their brain and heart instant gratification for the love they bestow. We all understand the need for human touch and attention.

In fact, that common impulse is the reason orphanage tourism is among the most gratifying and popular types of mission work. Orphan care is definitely what drew me to Haiti and my first experiences holding babies and toddlers in an orphanage is still seared in my memory as one of the more touching and memorable moments of my life.

I arrived in Haiti with a blank slate when it came to my opinion of orphanages. The many Biblical scriptures that advocated for orphan care gave the existing orphanages an immediate endorsement. For quite some time, I toyed with the idea of starting my own children's home (orphanage). The desperation and extreme poverty I witnessed was so intense, it sometimes felt that no matter what was done, there were always kids in desperate need of a safe place to go. My mother heart felt like it would rather burst than allow babies to be born into this world to suffer and not do something to gather them up and take care of them.

Over the next few years, I formed a strong opinion that swung in the opposite direction based on the more sinister sides I saw of these institutions. Admittedly, I have since lightened my stance a bit, knowing that most people involved in orphanages are doing the best they can. There is so much grey area that strict endorsements or condemnations can never be accurate. Condescension also never fixed anything, and there are no black and white solutions when faced with the kind of poverty one sees in Haiti. It's easy to stand on the sidelines and give advice and critiques. I have been the recipient of these kinds of judgements more often than I can count in my own line of work. And while we should always be rethinking how we are doing things and have a mandate to do so, finger wagging from the sidelines is very rarely a catalyst for change.

We can judge others on how they do ministry, but the real question is, what are *we* doing to make the orphan crisis better? Are we just critics? Or worse, are we participating in something quite possibly harmful? So what do I really think? What do I think is the best way to help kids who are in orphanages or kids at risk for being abandoned to orphanages? Let me try my best to explain.

James 1:27:
"Religion that God our Father accepts as pure and faultless is this: to look after orphans and widows in their distress and to keep oneself from being polluted by the world."

The above is just one of the many verses that evangelicals in America have hung their hat on. I understand why. It suggests a simple four-step solution for churches across America.

1. Find an orphanage in a poor foreign country.

2. Take up an offering.

3. Send the money.

4. Check the box that says, "We are Biblical Christians following the will of God to love people and care for orphans."

The problem is that it just isn't that simple. Don't I wish it were! It leaves out the human part of how the poor react to streams of income, how it incentivizes orphanages to exist, and how opening orphanages actually creates more orphans in hard places like Haiti. It leaves us uninformed and assuming that kids in orphanages are actual orphans. But it also gives us a false and dangerous sense of security that we are doing what we think we are doing. In reality, we could be (and most likely are) contributing to the problem. *We are funding the orphan crisis.*

A church might take it a step further and organize a mission to visit the orphanages the congregation supports. The senses are overwhelmed by the dozens and even hundreds of kids in the orphanages. For a week, the visitors hold babies and play with toddlers and tell each other how they wish they could take all the poor babies home with them. Like me when I tried to sign up for the NICU opportunity in college, orphanage tourists are filled with immediate gratification for their caring efforts. But then they hop on a plane and go home, adding to the cycle of abandonment already a staple in these vulnerable children's day to day lives.

The cycle does not end there. The next set of orphanage tourists will come the next week showering the kids with gifts and affection from another set of complete strangers whom they will never see again.

These orphanage visits make evangelical hearts swell with compassion. They pledge to give more money, and the extra cash offerings help the orphanage grow bigger. The orphanage adds twenty more beds. More children are relinquished by their parents, who hope the facility will give their kids a better shot at a prosperous life. Never mind the obvious moral and ethical concerns that arise, such as what becomes of kids who are raised in homes such as these? And is building a bigger facility a solution?

Many of us don't stop to think about how this situation came to be. Where do all these "orphans" come from? We say, "Well, isn't it better to fund an orphanage than to have a child die?" Absolutely it is. An orphanage would certainly be a good plan B and a great alternative to dying. But I would say that there is another way. The ultimate Plan A. And that is for children to stay with their mothers and fathers. I believe that this is where the church's generosity and efforts and heartbeat should lie. Not in supporting orphanages, but in supporting poor families through empowerment *so that their children don't have to become orphans.* Imagine the Good News that that would be to a poverty orphan:

You get to keep your mama.

Your mama is going to have enough money to send you to school and feed you.

You don't have to be abandoned.

This is the heart of the Orphan Gospel.

I'll repeat what I discuss in my memoir, *Shelley in Haiti:* More than 80% of kids in orphanages around the world have living parents. That's right: 80%. Poverty is the culprit. Lack of food and resources have led a desperate mother to an orphanage gate to do what she thought she could never bear to do. Her child will now be labeled "orphan." And she, the mother, will be written out of the story on Orphan Sunday and in the missions bulletin that goes out every Christmas. My heart aches that she is overlooked. Justice begs that we start to see her in this equation.

Let it sink in that the toddler whom you have just held for a week on a mission trip and promised to support through monthly donations is most likely a grieving mother's child.

Imagine that grief.

There is a story you don't know. That mother might have prayed daily that she would have enough money to keep and raise her child. I know this because I know how hard the poor pray. We offer only one solution for her. The worst possible outcome for mother and child is our only offering — separation and abandonment.

"Oh, but they will get adopted and have a much better life," one might say.

Another great plan B.

But in truth, great, irreparable psychological damage is often done to the child who has been abandoned and institutionalized. Adopting kids from hard places is not for the faint of heart. Wishing for the best from a tragic beginning is to be applauded, but the tragedy of losing one's mother and father always precedes adoption, and I, as an adoptive mother, would never say that the end justifies the pain of that loss. Add to that the fact that only a very small percentage of kids who are raised in institutions and orphanages are adopted, and that silver lining quickly fades. Adoption is beautiful and I am 100% behind it, but it certainly is not the solution to the orphan crisis. There are simply too many children, too much red tape in international adoption, and not enough willing families for that to be the solution that meets the need of the current crisis. There are about 32,000 documented children living in orphanages in Haiti. (There are most likely more because records may not account for those kids who have not been registered.) Yet according to the website *www.travel.state.gov*, only 178 Haitian children were adopted in 2016. In 2015, there were 143 completed adoptions assigned to the United States. The chances of being adopted from an orphanage are staggeringly low — about .5% per year. Again, I want to emphasize that I am 100% pro-adoption, but it is clear that this alternative is nowhere near enough of a solution given these numbers.

The mass of children — about 31,000 — who are left in orphanages and never find a forever family is not an acceptable outcome for me. Most people would agree that an orphanage should be, at best, a temporary home. In my experience, orphanages do not raise healthy and happy, well-adjusted and well-loved children.

The foster care system in the United States, which is considered to be a step up from orphanages, does not boast the best outcomes for children either. Shalita O'Neale, the founder and director of Hope Forward, Inc., states that in the U.S., roughly 50% of the homeless in America spent time in foster care. The percentage of foster children involved in the juvenile justice system for children with five or more foster placements can be upwards of 90% according to the Juvenile Law Center (JLC.org). The statistics of prisoners who were formerly foster children is also tragic. Foster care is deemed to be better than orphanages, but the outcomes for children raised in this system are bleak. Imagine how much less hope is in store for institutionalized kids in poor countries who have been cut off from familial ties and support. What will become of them as adults in the world?

For me, it's back to plan A.

Most kids who are raised in orphanages are not trained in any way that prepares them to be successful adults. My own Montessori training taught me the extreme importance and correlation between work and play and mimicking adults and the small window of time kids have to make the cerebral connections that set them up to be productive adults. Children raised in orphanages are very often undereducated, another sad paradox as many mothers and fathers relinquish their children naively believing the facility to be like a free boarding school that will provide that elusive education that they could never afford. Many children, especially those raised in orphanages run by non-Haitian nationals, are not even taught basic skills, such as how to cook a meal or clean a room. It is even more rare that they are taught a skill or trade that would empower them to earn a living and support themselves as adults.

Children who grow up in orphanages often become third-culture citizens, especially if the orphanage is run by foreigners. They exist halfway between their native culture and the culture of the people who raised them. With foreigners coming in and out of their lives on a weekly basis lavishing them with gifts that they didn't have to work for, a sense of entitlement takes them even further away from the reality that they will soon face — being forced out of the orphanage and expected to create a productive life.

Due to state laws in Haiti, orphanages must expel children at the age of eighteen, even though these "adults" often have no home to return to. (Family members are often reluctant to accept the burden of the responsibility for bringing them back into their homes.) Imagine being tossed into the streets of any city at eighteen without an adequate education and attempting to take care of yourself. Imagine not having the ability to form normal healthy bonds with caregivers and parental figures, now represented by bosses and employers, assuming a job is ever offered. Imagine your concept of a "family" when you want to start your own. Imagine coming from a background of emotional and physical abuse as is common in orphanages and trying to thrive in the real world with such a low sense of self-worth.

"Orphans" have been set up for failure. Despite the good intentions of charitable people who genuinely want to help, in many cases these children are worse off than they were before being abandoned to the orphanage. They have not been parented.

Social skills, kindness, helpfulness, emotional maturity, forgiveness, character development have all gone by the wayside. The consequences for individuals are obvious, yet society is also harmed.

I have seen it first-hand in my neighborhood. I have tried to hire kids who were raised in orphanages with very little success. The many children in Haiti who grow up as restaveks do much better. They at least have job skills and a work ethic. It is a cruel and embarrassing reality that they are often better prepared as adults in Haiti than kids raised in Christian orphanages. My experiences have testified to this. I have hired and worked with people from both backgrounds. The results speak clearly to me. Children raised in orphanages are overwhelmingly ill-equipped to succeed as adults.

We might wince at a poor child's needs and advocate that we can take care of the child so much better with the resources we have, but what price justifies the pain a mother endures in losing her child, and the child his mother? We are so often willing to contribute to meet her children's needs only if she abandons them. At what point is it better for a child to be institutionalized and abandoned than to be raised with a loving mother? Who makes that decision?

Unfortunately, and in their defense, orphanages are often a necessity in a place like Haiti. I have seen too many babies who are on death's doorstep but for the grace of an orphanage director who is willing to take the child in. So, let me be clear, I am not advocating that we ignore the horrendous circumstances children face just because I believe these facilities are imperfect. If an orphanage is the only immediate solution, then I'll take it. But as a person of faith, I know that this is the very *least* Christians and other generous, caring people can do.

So, what then is the solution?

Plan A. Parents must be empowered to support and keep their children.

Two things are most crucial for a parent to keep their children in a context like Haiti. *They need to have a job and they need for their children to go to school.* I have found that when those two criteria are met, the instances of child relinquishment plummet to the same levels as one might see in the USA. Parents overwhelmingly want to keep their children. But they want their children to have a future.

So what about those babies who are starving to death? Shouldn't we have orphanages for them?

There are fortunately better solutions than forcing a family apart!

New hybrid homes for children are springing up as nutrition centers. The idea is to work with families of starving children, who usually stay for a short time. The parents are involved in the recovery and taught what kinds of foods are best for overcoming malnutrition. These homes are a step in the right direction and are worthy of our attention and generosity.

Finding quality schools in Haiti to support and grow is another step in the right direction. It presents a solution without all the heartbreak of broken families. If every dollar that was spent on orphanages went to quality education, we might just see orphanages go extinct in our lifetime. For many parents, the hope for an education is the dream. The gospel that a child could get an education without losing his or her mother in the process is certainly "good news to the poor."

Lastly, the most crucial and final solution is jobs. It is what I have spent a decade pursuing in Haiti. When a parent has a job, they no longer need to depend on outside help to take care of their children. This is the final goal and the ultimate in empowerment. We encourage jobs for the poor when we buy items that are from developing countries that are produced following fair trade principles. We want people to be paid a fair wage in good working conditions and with the right support and tools to be successful. If every family in America bought at least one gift from Haiti per year, *it would change the nation*. Tourism also does much to contribute to job opportunities in a place like Haiti. Unfortunately, the country's political and economic problems make it hard to look past the bad press and see the beautiful beaches and mountains that Haiti boasts, but there is a dormant tourism industry waiting to emerge if the political situation can stabilize and security is established.

The Orphan Gospel is the hope that we, as the body of Christ, can see into the soul of a mother and exhaust every opportunity and possibility to help her before she is forced to relinquish her children. Orphanages should be the last resort. Jobs, education, and meeting immediate, crucial needs should be our focus. As a church, we can do better than offering support in the form of such a bitter pill. She should not have to give up her precious children in order for them to live.

SECTION 4

Good News to the Poor:
Creating Jobs as a Holy Practice

Proverbs 14:23
"All hard work brings a profit,
but mere talk leads only to poverty."

1. Job Creation

*M*any evangelical Christians might ask what job creation has to do with faith. We are so trained to separate the spiritual and the secular, as if God isn't the author of both. While the evangelical movement has done much to mobilize people to share the good news of a loving God who has come to have relationship with us (and that is GOOD news), it has also lost some valuable expressions of faith along the way. The New Testament church, for example, was known for its unbounded generosity. Today, it would be difficult to find a church that even partially resembles those tenets because of our independent lifestyles and corporate culture. Our churches, barely resembling Christianity in its infancy, are run like businesses on budgets and much less like the supernatural expression of God's love for people. A church picnic or ladies' Bible study is our idea of community. Trying to keep the food bank pantry stocked or tithes coming in to help the needy is often a challenge. Most of us forget how often "the poor" are mentioned in scripture and yet we obsess on other parts of our faith that have very little clear direction in the Bible.

One or two verses on morality, women in leadership, predestination, or spiritual gifts will easily split a church while caring for the poor, a clear mandate, goes unnoticed and unaddressed in our statements of theology. We focus so much on what *not* to do and which sins are the worst that we lose sight of the good we ought to be doing. "Loving one another" is the brush stroke that should paint a clear and concise summary of who we should be as people of God and Christ followers. How simple a mandate to us — just to love people.

Isaiah 58 is among my personal favorite chapters because it talks about the blessings that God is ready to pour out on us all if we are attentive to the poor and the needy. Indeed, poverty is one of the most talked-about topics in scripture, and in God's eyes (according to scripture) how a society treats the poor is an indicator of its morality. *Helping the poor reflects genuine faith.*

For churches that recognize the importance, caring for the poor is mostly characterized by contributing to orphanages, homeless shelters, food banks, short term missions trips, building homes, and more. These things are all commendable.

But what if caring for the poor meant acknowledging and offering that temporary reprieve from poverty while also getting people out of poverty — *forever*? What if full restoration is what God has in mind? Is that too much to hope for? When was the last time you saw a food bank get someone permanently out of poverty? When did giving someone money ever change a person's overall economic status? There is nothing wrong with charity, but could there be an even better solution to poverty alleviation? And could this solution also be considered an expression of faith? Is job creation a mission? Might business be more than just secular?

My mind has been converted to see *opportunity to work* as a holy endeavor in the fight against poverty. We are created to be productive, as our Maker also is productive and creative. We are, after all, made in His image. Here is what God had in mind when creating humankind:

The Lord God took the man and put him in the Garden of Eden to work it and take care of it.
Genesis 2:15

The first thing the Lord did was give humans a beautiful garden and the ability to be its caretakers. Work itself was, at that time, a blessing and gave purpose. It was, most likely, the bulk of Adam's daily activities.

Unfortunately, as the story goes, a series of nasty events turned things sour quickly and brought about the part of work that we are much more familiar with today.

Cursed is the ground because of you;
through painful toil you will eat food from it all the days of your life. It will produce thorns and thistles for you, and you will eat the plants of the field. By the sweat of your brow you will eat your food until you return to the ground.
Genesis 3:17-19

One of the curses of separation from God and how we were created is about doing work that is unproductive and laborious.

Nobody is more familiar with unproductive work than the poor. I have witnessed a woman in Haiti spend the entire day walking to a stream, filling jugs with water, and then carrying them home on her head so her family could bathe and hydrate. I've seen other women scrimp and save just to buy beans and then spend the whole day preparing the food, while hand-washing the precious few clothes she has until her knuckles bleed. She doesn't have a paying job, but no one can say she doesn't work. Her work is largely unproductive. It keeps her from dying of thirst or starvation, but hardly gets her ahead in life.

In fact, by definition, the wealthier you are, the less you must labor to stay alive.

The curse of Eden seems to be the fact that the work is rendered unproductive, futile, and toilsome and the poor do not come into the blessing of prosperity as a result of it.

So how do we bring the good news of productive and rewarding work? How can the curse of poverty be broken? Giving the poor a place where they can start to reap the results of their labor is in every way a mandate for my faith and a spiritual practice. If we can consider a charitable handout of rice a spiritual practice, than surely empowering people to grow their own rice could be deemed heavenly. It has been said many times, but this mindset remains powerful: Give a person a fish and you feed them for a day, teach them to fish and…a profound change occurs. Taking it a step further, showing them the way to the market where they can sell their fish is where the most magic happens. The cycle of poverty and unproductive toil can end and it is where we begin to truly help the poor permanently through empowerment.

I hope the leap from orphan care to job creation is forming a connection in your mind. Think of the amount of money donated to various charities over the years. What if that same amount of money had been used to create and provide jobs so that parents could feed, clothe, and educate their children? How much further would that money have gone? And how much more independent and empowered would the recipients be by now?

Of course there is always a time for giving, but my memoir *Shelley in Haiti* narrates the painful lessons I learned in my early years when I believed more heavily in charity as the solution to problems. Merely writing a check may salve the conscience of the donor, but it may not have much of a lasting impact or help another human in the way that was hoped. Jobs are the remedy, an enduring cure for the ills that afflict the poor. This truth is universal. And this truth is no less spiritual.

2. Expecting Excellence and Moving Beyond Charity

*W*hen we began making recycled cereal box beads in the early years, I still had a "charity mindset" in how I approached the artisans I worked with. I accepted anything the artisans made for me to sell and relied on sympathy from the buyer to buy it. A good heartwarming Facebook post did wonders to sell jewelry made out of trash! This worked at the beginning and during the time of the earthquake, but I quickly realized that if we didn't start producing things of quality that people loved, we would fail: We'd be just another short-lived mission wanting to be a hero in Haiti.

Originally, the artisans made dirty, misshapen beads. I tried to teach them the importance of quality, asking for a shiny, perfectly round bead to be made from the recycled boxes we used. They largely ignored me. They could make about 150 beads a day, and half the beads couldn't be used because they were so badly made. Necklaces were getting uglier and uglier and the beads were awful and unraveling.

I finally had enough. I knew that if I didn't demand a higher quality, all would be in vain. I had to put my money where my mouth was.

I called everyone in to work one day and had them roll beads. I announced at the beginning of the day that we were going to be inspecting beads for quality and they would need to have a certain quality standard in order to continue to work. At the end of the day we examined the beads to see who would pass the new quality standards I had clearly spelled out. Only twenty or so artisans made beads we could use. The rest of them were literally killing the business opportunity with their sloppy workmanship.

I laid off forty poor Haitian parents that day. It was a bold move. It felt counter-intuitive and was one of the hardest things I have ever had to do, but I knew I had to draw a tough line. *I had to expect from them what I knew they were capable of.* The twenty remaining artisans were in shock. Yet, the next day their beads were of the best quality I had ever seen. And the day after that several of the artisans I had let go came back, each with a handful of beautiful beads to show me. I hired them back into the fold as well.

In the weeks after, I was able to rehire almost every single person who had been let go that day, because something magical happened. They rose to the challenge. They became more than they thought they could be. Having high standards was achievable. It also brought a dignity to the workplace. Pity purchases and low standards are only a small step above charity.

I still have plenty of quality issues that come up in our artisan center, but to this day, we have the best cereal box beads in the country. I can actually look at a paper bead and tell if it came from our artisan center or not and the bead quality has never deteriorated since. It was a lesson that I learned early on about high expectations being a tool for empowerment. When a person in our artisan facility makes a necklace poorly or doesn't glaze a mug to standard, I ask myself if I am empowering them in their job to let it slide. The answer is a resounding no. Setting the bar high is paramount to future success — not only for them, but for the company's ability to provide more jobs. They are more than capable of attaining excellence, and expecting less from people who are economically challenged is falling into a trap of pity and piousness and condescension. In short, it is demeaning to them. By expecting more, you show you truly care more about their future success and are willing to be the catalyst to help them reach their highest potential.

3. Job Creation Recipe

*W*orking in a country like Haiti, it is hard to find a tried and true recipe for success. I have consulted with many veteran business professionals with the hope of learning how to do what I do better. In turn, other ambitious entrepreneurs have brought their manuals, ideas, business plans, case studies, and advertisement schemes to me for my opinion and review.

Frankly, it makes me feel sheepish, because in most ways those same people asking me for advice are so much more professional and prepared than I ever was. When I began, I didn't have a clue what I was stepping into. I had no business or marketing background. No design background. I didn't know the first thing about budgets, costs, spreadsheets, or margins. So it is often amusing to watch people stop, scratch, and then tilt their heads to the side to comprehend. "You had no business background?" they question me.

"Correct. When I began I had absolutely no experience in the field. At university I studied German and linguistics before becoming a full-time mom."

"German?…"

"I know. It doesn't make sense."

"But…"

"It's amazing where passion can take you!"

For all my misgivings about my background and business acumen, I learned through experience, from being on the ground and reacting to the paradoxical and, at times, infuriating circumstances. Trial and error may not be textbook, but apparently it is an astounding teacher, because through the years I've watched many good-hearted people arrive with big business plans and great ideas only to fail. Ultimately, what they created didn't make sense in the wild-card context of Haitian society. Being untrained, I may have actually had an advantage because I didn't know what business was "supposed" to look like.

For example, well thought-out business plans formulated by professionals behind corporate tables and sitting in air-conditioned rooms don't account for the real-life struggles of the poor in Haiti. How do they show up on time when they have never had to keep track of a clock? How do they maintain hygiene at work when they have only ever used the bathroom on the ground? How do our most educated managers do their jobs well when they can't realistically do math above the fourth-grade level? How does a woman focus on work when her baby is left in the house alone because she couldn't find childcare and still had to come to work in order to be able to eat? The best laid plans will need to be adapted into an unpredictable context like Haiti. The ability to pivot and use a backup plan when supplies can't be found, internet goes down, or a hurricane wreaks havoc on your town is the foundation for success. It is no small feat to be able to train people to work in these conditions and then also try to compete on the global market. Sometimes it is more than daunting. Sometimes it feels impossible.

Three determining factors have made the difference between those I have watched succeed and those who have packed up and left after just a few years. The three key factors for me are presence, passion, and purpose.

4. Presence, Passion, and Purpose

I met an intelligent and compassionate young woman with all the business know-how you could ever hope for. After two years of trying to build a business in the handicraft sector she left Haiti. She had thought out every conceivable hurdle she might face, but for her the enterprise was merely a stepping-stone. A line on her resume. A Peace Corps experience that she hoped would impress others in her future climb up the corporate ladder.

How nice for her that she could simply pull up stakes and leave. Meanwhile, what about the Haitian women who had taken part in the program, believing they were climbing a staircase to a better life themselves? They tumbled back to poverty and frustration. In some ways, this kind of short-term dedication is worse than doing nothing. So much trust is left to rot on the bedrock of dreams deferred.

Presence is the difference between success and failure here. I have never seen an organization succeed in Haiti that is run from a distance. One of the biggest problems I see in the nonprofit world is the disconnect between what board members and leadership in the states are dreaming, and what is going on in Haiti. Visiting this nation several times a year and picking up some artisan's work to share with friends and family is not presence. To succeed you must be on the ground where you gain wisdom, sharpen your local street smarts, and develop a connection to the Haitian people. That can't happen from abroad. Presence distinguishes a visionary or founder from one who is not willing to get his or her hands in the dirt and do the real work. It requires blood, sweat, and tears. It can be painful. But the willingness to put in the time creates a solidarity with the poor that is crucial to Haiti and the company's longevity on the island. I lived in Haiti full-time for almost a decade. It has shaped me and made the difference in what I do. It has connected me forever to the people and the pain that I see around me. We have forged a bond that keeps me continually connected. Today this proves a challenge as I have needed to be stateside more for my children's schooling and for the growth of the warehouse portion of the business. The lack of constant presence in Haiti has definitely caused some difficulty, but the staff I have on the ground who spent so much time with me working side by side makes it still work for us.

I started the nonprofit Apparent Project for one reason: I was *passionate* about helping mothers support their children. It was a calling born from a revelation I had of the pain women experience when they must relinquish their beloved children to orphanages simply because they can't afford to properly feed and house them. Their sacrifice stirred something so deep in me that it became my identity. Give up when the going gets tough? Impossible. It has become my calling. It is what drives and sustains me when I have been robbed, lied to, disappointed, threatened, can't pay the bills, and am sweating and sick in a country that seems to have been cursed. If I were to falter, all I'd need to do is look at my own children and be grateful that I have never had to make a decision as hard as many Haitian mothers face every day.

What's your purpose? That's the question I was asked over and over by a business consultant who had traveled some distance to spend a week with me in Haiti. He asked me if all my employees knew what the company's purpose was. He told me that we needed to have our purpose stamped on our hearts and engrained in the minds of our Haitian employees so that whenever someone walked in the door and asked what we were doing, everyone could exhale the same words: "We are working to be able to take care of our children and to create opportunity for other mothers to do the same." Our purpose keeps us focused on who we are and why we need to continue when the going gets tough.

I was not put on this earth to be a manufacturer of mugs or a peddler of paper jewelry. My purpose is job creation in whatever form it can come. I was called to give hope and opportunity, and to be an advocate for moms who wish to raise their children with dignity. This is my purpose and it is my company's purpose. Every morning I wake up and I know that this is why I am here.

Innocent as Doves,
Wise as Serpents:
Cultural Considerations

Proverbs 19:29
"Whoever is patient has great understanding."

A beloved humanities professor I studied with in college had a mantra that has stuck with me through the years. He repeatedly urged us to "define and describe."

"Be slow to judgement, be slow to criticism. Observe." He taught us. Our first instinct and human nature is to jump to judgment and form opinions without giving ourselves time to really understand and process the facts. He challenged us to slow down and truly see and understand before we came to judgement or criticism (let alone solutions!). As a university student in my twenties, I had no idea how important his words would later be for me.

Define and describe. Taking time to observe, listen, and question experiences is what I have been challenged to do these past years in Haiti. My own responses to poverty have been typical: I arrived and wanted to jump right in and start fixing things. The poverty and problems scream for immediate attention. Every day is a crisis. Self-restraint is tough. Eventually and inevitably, the impulse to jump in without first understanding overwhelms and can cause burnout because largely, *our solutions don't work without adjustments to the cultural context*. Not when we don't fully understand the problems or the back story on the issues we are addressing. Helping in Haiti without understanding it in context would be like a counselor giving advice without first listening to a client's story or a doctor prescribing medicine without the medical records. The first step is this: Stop, learn, and observe. Real solutions only follow *hard-earned* understanding. One of the first things I learned about Haiti is to not assume that I understand what people's reasons are and, even more importantly, not to pass judgment about someone's capabilities based on things that they do that I don't understand. We have in our American culture an undergirding of stability that Haitians do not have the privilege of relying on. Comparing our way of doing things with theirs misses the point. While we grew up using can openers, they learned how to open cans with a knife. Both ways work. We obviously feel like we have the "right tool" but it is a tool that is not accessible to them. The knife works in their context. And if we hand them a can opener, they will go back to using the knife. Their way works for them. We must change our mentality to understand theirs. In a culture where tomorrow is not promised to you and physical belongings can be wiped out by rains, theft, or being lost in other ways, today is ALL that matters. Making choices for the future is a luxury that most do not entertain. We would be wise to take the time to understand what motivates people, what fears they have, and what has led them to do things the way they do them before we are so bold as to try to change things we don't understand — *even if it would make their lives better.* Here are some things that I have wrestled with in my efforts to work with the poor in the job creation sector.

1. Secrecy is King

The wounds of slavery on a people are profound. Research indicates trauma can actually be passed down in a person's DNA. When everything you have is taken away from you by slavery or when poverty is the water you swim in, you learn to protect any little thing you *do* care about with all you have. You tell no one of the good things in your life. No good news dares to be shared. You can't risk losing anything else or drawing attention. You can't risk someone else knowing and taking it away from you.

I have made so many social blunders surrounding this concept and find that I still have much to learn.

Sonia comes to me in my office and bends down and whispers something unintelligible.

"I can't hear you," I say back in Kreyol. "Why don't you just say what you have to say?"

"Can we go on the balcony and talk?" she whispers again.

I'm a little annoyed by the disturbance. But I get up and go with her to the balcony.

"I need black bag," she says to me when we get out there.

"A *black* bag?" I'm surprised and wonder why we had to go to the balcony for this.

I had just given a few of the artisans with kids some diapers and onesies that had come in as donations.

"I need a bag for the clothes," she said again.

"Can't you just put it in your purse?" I whispered loudly enough for her to hear.

"No. I need a plastic bag. Black if you have it."

So specific.

I learned over the years, in moments like this, that you can't give anything to anyone without giving them a way to hide what it is. "Cache" — to HIDE in Kreyol. It's an important word to know. No one can know their business. The risk is too great to get stolen from or harassed for what they have. To be perceived as a "have" instead of a "have-not" is detrimental.

I find a plastic bag stuffed somewhere in the corner of my office. It's not black, but it will do. I get tired of the game. Why does everything have to be so guarded and secret? If you get a passport, tell no one. If you get money to rent a house, tell no one. If you buy land, definitely tell no one.

It makes it hard to get the success stories that are so coveted by our buyers. So many times, clients will come to me and ask me for accounts of our artisans' successes. It's awesome for marketing when people know that their purchases are making a difference in people's lives. I stutter and try to explain that good news is hard to come by. I have to pry it out of them. They guard it fiercely. And they certainly don't want their success plastered on Facebook. People in their neighborhood will see. Many in Haiti might not have food or clothes, but oddly enough, they all have a cell phone and

Facebook. Even when I post pictures of myself with artisans on my own social media, they tell me that sometimes they get a backlash. It's worth mentioning that short term trips to Haiti and the pictures that get posted on social media from those trips may also have ramifications we know nothing about. Discretion is king.

The notion of a "secrecy culture" can and should be understood lest we do harm when we intend to help. Handing out gifts, clothes, bags of rice, jobs; celebrating accomplishments, giving awards, taking pictures, making personal information private — all must be treated with utmost care. We may never know what our Haitian friends endure long after we are gone because of the way we handle the confidentiality of their lives.

2. The Thief

I woke up to a flurry of activity. My house is inside the walls of the artisan facility and there are always people around. In my house, outside my house, in the yard — always people. It is never boring. The hyper atmosphere and chatter made me realize that something had happened.

"What's going on out there?" I said to my security guard who was sitting just outside my door.

"They got a thief," he replied unemotionally. The drama had long since been lost on the security force. "He's just outside the gate."

Of course, my curiosity and obligation as owner of the company impelled me to investigate, so I walked up the sloped corridor to the front of the artisan facility and went out into the street. A mob had gathered.

There in the dirt was a young man, stripped naked, dead, lying face up in the unpaved road.

Sometime during the night, he had been stoned to death right there in the intersection in front of the house.

No one knew who he was. He wasn't from the neighborhood. He had a big boulder of a rock placed on top of his chest. I wasn't sure if this was so that he wouldn't roll away or so that cars would see him and not run him over. I tried not to look at his face. I still had enough PTSD issues from the earthquake that looking at dead bodies too closely was not a good idea. I had learned to be a bit more protective of myself.

"Why was he killed?" I asked my neighborhood friends.

"He was probably a thief," they said matter-of-factly.

"Wow. That's the penalty for stealing!" I thought.

I remembered back to my first days in Haiti when a laptop had gone missing. I knew who had taken it and I wanted to go to the police. I remember in a conversation discussing it angrily with several other artisans. "He is a *thief*! I know he *stole* it!" Their faces showed just how hard those words were to them. Those were two words I learned over time never to use again. *Thief* and *Steal*. An accusation like that can get you killed.

It's not uncommon for justice to be served on the spot. With inadequate and underpaid police presence, people are known to take justice into their own hands if they want to be assured of it.

Accusations are not taken lightly. These people don't have the luxury of a fair trial and adequate representation in a court of law. Even an accusation that leads to an arrest might be the end of someone.

It is a serious matter to be accused or to accuse and one that should not be taken lightly.

3. Dignity

$\mathcal{D}$ignity is a big deal in a poverty culture. Self-esteem is a battle and any accomplishments are guarded fiercely. What seems like arrogance and laziness to me sometimes has much more behind it than I would have ever realized when I first started working in Haiti.

One of my American staff was angry with a Haitian manager.

"I just asked him to help carry the empty boxes into the storage area," he said to me. "He wouldn't do it. He's so lazy."

Our Haitian manager had been obviously avoiding the task at hand and made a few excuses as to why he wasn't going to help and quickly got another worker to do the job. Education is a badge of honor in Haiti. It is such an accomplishment to finish high school, let alone college. There is a cultural understanding that upon receiving their diplomas, they have also now "graduated" from menial tasks and manual labor. There are plenty of people in the country who can do those jobs! Graduates see themselves as above those tasks and their own self esteem will not allow them to "stoop" to the level they were at before.

Our American mindset is so different from this. We watch shows like "Undercover Boss" with tears in our eyes and celebrate leadership that is willing to get down and dirty on the same level as the lowest paid workers. As Christians, we preach the message of the cross and the way of Jesus, who humbled himself to walk among us. Our culture (hopefully) values the hard work of the blue-collar worker. Most of us have been there and done that kind of work and don't feel that we are above it. We don't have maids and servants (most of us) and even those of us with college degrees find ourselves at home cleaning toilets and washing our own dishes.

Not so in Haiti. People with money and education always have employees for these kinds of domestic jobs. It is considered demeaning and disrespectful to make a person who has educational status do work that is beneath them. This has been beyond frustrating for me (coming from my cultural background, remembering when I was a maid in a hotel, a waitress, and a nanny) to have to cave and surrender to this cultural reality. I am not going to change the culture. I need to work with it. And I need to understand it even when I want to judge it and, quite frankly, don't like it. It looks and smells like arrogance to me, but if I challenge it, I am eroding the little bit of self-respect and self-esteem that these individuals may have realized for their hard work and accomplishments. It is not a battle I am going to win — nor should I try to fight.

4. Initiative

*T*he past still haunts Haiti. The people were oppressed and abused and the generational scars from generations ago still carry on. Their forefathers trapped in slavery were taught to do exactly what they were told. No more and no less. Our American culture values self-starters and people with initiative but in the context of Haiti, workers often won't go beyond exactly what they are told to do. It simply isn't worth the risk for them and isn't the cultural norm. They do not want to do the wrong thing and fear making mistakes.

This can be frustrating from an outsider's perspective, but over the years I have tried to understand the "why" behind it all. The penalty for making mistakes has historically been out of proportion to the error and so people learn that even if they see something they could do, it is not worth the risk.

Imagine a child from a rough home who gets severely punished for his mistakes. He's going to try to stay under the radar, do exactly what is expected, and leave it at that. It simply isn't safe to do more. In the workplace, job descriptions become a sort of bible and if it's not in the job description, it's not part of the job. I have had to learn to adapt and modify each job description to be sure it encompasses all that I want an employee to do. I recently asked an employee to send me a weekly report and then complained to him for never communicating with me. His response was straightforward. "You told me to do my job. I do my job. You never told me I was supposed to talk to you. That's not in my job description." In our American culture, we value workers who will see a need and take care of things, who will go the extra mile. We expect that any good worker would go above and beyond to prove their worth, get a raise, etc. The more I understand the background behind the why, the less frustrating this is and the more I can adapt and create a workforce culture that feels safe where they know they will not be punished or humiliated for mistakes or taking risks. Getting to the root of the issue and creating a safe place to learn together is the first step to allow our artisans to bloom and grow.

5. I Am the Foreigner

*O*ffice supplies are expensive in Haiti. The thought of spending the little money we have on over a hundred envelopes more than twice a month made me cringe. While most of our artisans are now paid with direct deposit, many still get paid in cash. My environmental nerves are irritated and besides the cost, the thought of wasting the paper on envelopes bothers me, too.

Dignity and secrecy. It was something I kept having to get used to. Handing cash out without putting it in an envelope was demeaning to the artisans. The envelope communicated respect and protected them from eyes in the room who were assessing how much money they were being paid. It was a losing battle for me.

In the end I have to realize that I am the guest in this country. I need to figure out how things are done here and try to understand and adapt. People don't like to follow what they don't understand. If it doesn't make sense to us, *believe me* when I say that it is *we* who do not understand something. I promise that in time, if you find yourself in this kind of situation in a foreign country and you stick around long enough, you will have your "aha" moment and want to kick yourself for not seeing things their way much sooner! People do what works for them. The trick is to find out *why* it is the way that they have chosen.

6. Education

*W*hile I firmly believe in education as a solution in Haiti, I think it is imperative to acknowledge that we probably don't understand the huge difference between school in America and school in a developing country like Haiti. It is super important to describe the situation and understand what education is like for the average poor person to best know how to support educational initiatives — which I highly recommend doing as part of orphan prevention initiatives. I suggest anyone who is funding schools or sponsoring a child's education to do due diligence and be sure that those dollars are going to truly help students in Haiti with quality education, as much as is possible.

We're back in my living room in the heat of the summer months with a fan turned on full blast. My couch only seats five, but six women have squished themselves in on the sofa cushions — a rare treat for many of the artisans who don't have the luxury of couches in their homes. All of them have worked with me for a long time, most of them for more than six years. I bought hot ham pizzas and cold Haitian Cokes from the café that is part of the Papillon business compound.

I invited them over to talk about several issues that I still felt like I didn't understand even after almost a decade in country. The school system was on my mind. Several of the ladies, including Sonia and Makilene, have more than four children, and the burden of sending their children to school is relentless. Books, uniforms, test fees, tuition, and everything else involved in sending a child to school is too much of a burden for a poor mother. Multiply this by four or five children, and it is more than their salaries can support, even with relatively well-paying jobs from me. I wanted to understand their situation better.

Sonia started off by explaining her situation. Last year, Sonia, who makes more than double the minimum wage, still couldn't afford to buy all the books required after paying tuition for her four kids, so two of them had to go without the necessary materials. Her voice cracked when she told me how the teacher beat her son for not having his school supplies. Sonia said it was all her fault for not having the money. Another time she was late in paying and the teacher humiliated her son in front of the class, telling him to leave immediately because his tuition was delinquent. Her son stood to leave, but apparently hadn't moved fast enough. The teacher pushed her eleven-year-old son toward the door, and he fell, splitting his head on the concrete.

Tears streamed down her face as Sonia recounted to me this painful memory. Her son had come home covered in blood and a light tan Band-Aid, made obviously for Caucasian skin, plastered to his forehead. Her son didn't want to talk about it because his family's financial situation had embarrassed him. Worse, he didn't want to go to school again.

It's shocking, really. This is education?

Elimern was sitting next to Sonia quietly until I asked if anyone else had also experienced bad things when their kids went to school. She nodded at me and began to tell the story of her daughter, Yveline, in the fifth grade. Yveline had gone to school that past month and apparently hadn't been sitting with the correct posture. The teacher grabbed the skin on the back of her arms and twisted it in a horrendous pinch until Yveline screamed out in pain. The principal, hearing the commotion, came to the classroom asking what the matter was.

The teacher bent down and whispered to Yveline, "If you say anything you won't ever pass the fifth grade. Ever."

Yveline stifled her cry and wiped the tears. Her body straightened up into the correct posture and she went right to work. Her voice was not heard that day. Or many days after. The system is such that the independently run schools do what they want, teach what they want, charge what they want, discipline the way they want, and are not held accountable to enforced standards. Unfortunately, physical punishment and flat out physical abuse is still much the norm in public and private schools in Haiti.

Richard is repeating the ninth grade. He is now nineteen years old, but the poverty that he was born into has not made it easy to pay for school every year. Many years he was forced to drop out simply because his mother didn't have money. But last year was different. Richard was lucky enough to get into one of the few state-sponsored schools, with the relief of the free tuition. As is often the case, last year there were teacher strikes because of lack of government funding. Even the government in Haiti struggles to pay the bills. Every day during the month of

November, he would wake up at 6 a.m., put his school uniform on, and take the tap-tap to school. Upon arrival, he would find a classroom full of students, but no teacher. Day after day this went on. Students would continue to come, for fear of missing out and the consequences that would happen if they were caught absent. Eventually enough school had been missed that they would not be able to pass their exams. They would have to repeat the year. A year of school can easily be lost by a teacher strike, and kids get further and further behind. His state-sponsored school didn't end up being quite the blessing he had hoped for. At this rate, Richard will be in his mid-twenties before he finishes high school. His story is not unusual.

Classroom grade levels are not based on age but rather knowledge level, so it is possible to have a classroom full of eight and nine-year-olds with a few teenagers and adults in the mix at a first, second, or third grade level. People do what they can, when they can, and they press on. Few make it to the coveted graduation equivalent to high school called "Philo." But those who do still have an impossible mountain to climb ahead of them, as there are very few jobs even for high school graduates.

Going on to university is even more rigorous. It is a wonder Richard doesn't just drop out already. I'm sure it can seem like a hopeless situation for most who are in it — and certainly for those of us who are trying to fund it. Some people, knowing there might not be a job at the end of it all, still press on just for the sake of dignity. As discussed in earlier chapters, education is an honor. It is unfortunate that even those with the elusive diplomas and degrees have a hard time finding adequate employment at the end of such an uphill struggle.

Still, education is seen by most as the only real hope out of poverty. Other than a visa stamp in their passports, it is really the only hope. Even if it is faint.

Motivated much the same as churches and orphanages, the decentralized and loosely governed schools of Haiti are a huge recipient of foreign dollars, making them susceptible to pervasive corruption. Haiti is the land of school sponsorship. Years ago, before I came to live in Haiti, I sponsored a child through a well-known and reputable school sponsorship organization. I put the child's portrait on my fridge and felt bad about how few letters I wrote. At the same time, I wondered what the back story was. Was this really a child in need? What happened if she dropped out of school? What happened if she died? Was I the only sponsor? What kind of education was she getting? Although I was eager to be part of a solution, these questions nagged at me. I never really knew if my dollars were making a difference.

Later, I learned that children in Haiti are well aware of sponsors. In fact, it has become so much a way of life that they find it "normal" to have one. It is part of their life plan.

"What do you want to be when you grow up?" I ask Makenson one day as we walk down the dusty road. He is the second of seven kids, an eleven-year-old who so far has only made it to the second grade.

A goat runs ahead of us, bleating and kicking up dust, and almost gets hit by a car. We cover our eyes until the dust settles, then he looks up at me.

"I want to find a sponsor and go to school and become a doctor," he says, his broken tooth poking through his huge grin.

The "sponsor" has become a common ray of hope for Haitians. For better or worse, they have become dependent on foreigners to find their place in the world because they cannot rely on their own government or parents, who are poor. Wouldn't it be amazing if their parents could have jobs enough to break the cycle of dependency and allow them the dignity of providing for their own children?

Today in Haiti, the education system is built mostly with privately owned schools which are partially or entirely funded by foreign money. A lack of government-enforced regulation has allowed these schools to become business opportunities, and many of them don't even have qualified administrators or teachers. Opening a school is easy. Several houses in my neighborhood have transformed from personal residences into schools just by adding an outdoor space that can hold desks and benches and chalkboards. All that is required is for the owner of the house to put together a flyer advertising the school and hire someone (qualified or not) to be the teacher. Whether or not it is legally recognized is often overlooked. Getting legal paperwork when necessary is usually just a matter of filing a few papers. The poor families in my area will see the ad for the new neighborhood school and be willing to pay $25-$40 per month, plus all school supplies and uniforms, for each child enrolled. This is a huge sacrifice for a poor family, and even more so because they have no idea if their kids are getting an education worth that sacrifice, or indeed any education at all.

There is little published accountability information to indicate which schools are good schools, so it is not difficult for independently run school owners to make a few extra bucks off the trusting and hopeful parents in the area. Students are supposed to take government tests several times a year to advance to the next grade level. However, unlike schools in America that receive better ratings based on higher tests scores, and are incentivized by those scores, schools in Haiti are often incentivized financially if a child does not pass and is required to repeat and pay for the same grade twice.

Couple this with the almighty American dollars pouring in for education and it is not hard to see how it could be very easy for corruption to settle in.

Even with the best intentions and school administrators who have their hearts set on educating kids well as their primary mission, it still hard to get basic quality education.

Richard, who was still struggling to finish high school, was at my house and noticed the globe. It was the first time he had seen a globe. We started looking at it together and I asked him to point out Haiti. He spun the globe around and around twenty times before he finally gave up. I grabbed the globe and stopped the spinning just about where Florida was. My finger drew a line down to a tiny island just below.

"Ah! Li petit!"

"Yes, it is small!" I laughed at his shocked face. He had no idea how small his country was in the world.

He asked me where the United States was. I showed him. He was shocked by its size compared to Haiti. Our conversation progressed from the geography of the world to the solar system. He asked about the sun and moon. I made a fist to show him where the moon was and circled it around the globe, as a way of demonstrating how the moon revolves around the earth. He had no idea about orbiting planets.

Richard then made another fist. "This is the sun," he said.

I laughed. "No. The sun is much bigger."

How much bigger, he asked?

I looked around and pointed outside at my Toyota 4Runner in the driveway. "That is the sun. That's how much bigger the sun is than the earth."

He almost fell over.

The rest of the evening was spent explaining how the earth orbited around the sun and that made up a year and how the earth rotated on its axis and that made up a day. My grade-school kids knew more astronomy and were more informed about the world than Richard, who was in high school.

My point is not simply to be critical. The quality of the education system in Haiti must be addressed if Haiti can hope to change. Poorly taught students become poor teachers. Lack of government funding for education leaves the methods of teaching and the textbooks behind current thought. Teachers themselves may or may not have qualifications to teach. The method of education is mostly rote memory with little emphasis on problem solving or critical-thinking skills. Even the best schools in Haiti, including the ones I sent my kids to, have teachers who would never be qualified to teach in the United States.

So, what's the point then? What does critiquing the school systems have to do with orphan prevention? Primarily because foreigners fund it and because I believe so strongly that quality education is one of the keys to orphan prevention, we have a duty as we finance schools to expect and look for the quality education that the Haitian people deserve. When people ask me what Haiti needs and how to prevent child relinquishment, I can confidently say jobs and education. The next step is to make sure that our dollars support good fair jobs and good educations. The fact that most schools are funded largely by American dollars puts us right in position to do something about it. We have the responsibility if we are the ones sending the money. We have influence. And now we know. You and I know that we need to do better at educational initiatives for them to be "good news" to the poor and a key to orphan prevention.

I have unshakable hope that education can and will get better. And I believe that more than anything, education and jobs are the hope for real change out of poverty in Haiti.

In the mid-1970s my mother was a military wife who proudly followed my father to South Korea where he was stationed. At the time, the military did not want families to join servicemen because of the harsh third-world conditions that plagued the nation. Mom, undeterred, not only went to South Korea to be with my father, but did so with my brother, at the time an infant.

Nearly forty years later, the first time Mom visited me in Haiti, she said, "This reminds me of South Korea in the '70s."

Today, South Korea is a modern country with skyscrapers, neon lights, and the latest technology. The profound improvements occurred *in one generation*. I want to believe the same transformation is possible in Haiti. When we first started working with artisans rolling beads and making jewelry, I was in desperate need of higher-level managers to help me out. Within the ranks of bead rollers, we identified Shirley, a small, fifteen-year-old girl who spoke English. Shirley was quickly promoted to an assistant position and has continued to grow with the company. She is now a beautiful twenty-five-year-old wife and adoptive mother and has succeeded in several roles within the company, including production manager for all of Papillon. Why has she done so well?

Shirley's mother had the opportunity to send her to a local missionary school, the TLC Barefoot School, that taught kids from the poorest Haitian communities in a progressive-style educational setting where students learned English and critical-thinking skills. Shirley's quality education was obvious when we discovered how adept she was at problem solving, how she spoke impeccable English, and how she conducted herself comfortably with visiting American tourists. It made her the perfect candidate for upward mobility.

Shirley was not necessarily more intelligent than the other artisans. She had simply been given the opportunity for a good education and was able to develop her raw talents into polished skills, something most Haitians will never have the opportunity to do.

Apparent Project, a nonprofit that I helped found, has started a preschool and grade school that provides quality education for many of our artisan's children. Due to their age and lack of education in their formative years, many of our artisans may never have the ability to grow past being a jewelry maker, but their children, through the power of quality education, could have the opportunity to become whatever they aspire to be. Schools like TLC and Apparent Project and many more are providing hope in this area.

Missionaries come by the droves to teach vacation Bible school, offer medical clinics, hand out food and toys, and play with the children at orphanages. I long for the day when as much effort goes into bringing educators who could provide seminars to train teachers in new classroom methods and learning styles. This would end the emphasis on rote memorization and corporal punishment. In their place would be lessons in problem solving and constructive ways to motivate children without fear tactics.

The issue is allocation of funds. Just as I wish that for every dollar a church spends on orphan care, they would also put a dollar toward orphan prevention and quality education, I suggest the same amount donated for student sponsorships be matched for teacher development. This adjustment, I believe, would bring about radical change and put a huge dent in the number of children being relinquished and abandoned by their parents because of poverty. In my dreams I see a huge mega-orphanage — enough to house 200 children with a bright orange sign on the door that says, "Out of Business." Even better, I would love to see it turn into a well-funded and well-run school. I pray that the American church and other donors across the globe can be so aggressive toward orphan prevention that they make orphanages naturally obsolete. To allow a child to stay with his mother — that is good news to the poor.

SECTION 6

Be the Good News Where You Are: Living Out Heaven on Earth

Matthew 6:10
"Your kingdom come, your will be done,
on earth as it is in heaven."

1. Where Grace Fits In

I Corinthians 1:25
*"For the foolishness of God is wiser than human wisdom, and the
weakness of God is stronger than human strength."*

After all this talk about understanding and wisdom and
learning and observing, the truth is that we can really never
know what we are doing as foreigners in a context like Haiti or
another country or community like it. Our hearts long to help,
and we feel discouraged with all the information we get about
how what we are doing is wrong. Let me suggest that as people
of faith, we have a higher wisdom and a higher understanding
that we can lean into. The reality that God is alive and speaking to us, to them, and is moving in the world makes us all just
participants in the great story that He is crafting. And His story
is one of Grace. Let me tell a few stories as to how I have seen
this play out in my own life in Haiti.

Angelo
Poverty does not usually bring out the best in people. When
people grow up without even their basic needs being met, that

emotional trauma impacts every part of their lives. Many of our artisans have suffered starvation, abuse, the death of a child, and ongoing daily oppression. Any one of those things would be enough to have an American signed up for therapy for life. As much as we teach our artisans to roll beads, make pottery, and learn life skills, it can't be overlooked that a business that exists primarily for job creation instead of profits will spend a lot of time working on developing people into a deeper understanding of the world around them and how to live better in it. Healing their hurts is also a big part of what we want to do.

A few of my lead staff and I were talking one day. Angelo, one of our top Haitian male employees, who was a key manager for production and now heads up our work at the U.S. Embassy, was disgruntled and angry. He didn't feel valued for the work he was doing, and he didn't trust the company had his best interests in mind. It hurts to try so hard to help and continually have my motives questioned. But it was not unusual for our artisans to mistrust, given the history of abuse and unfairness they experienced from foreigners in Haiti. Over time, Angelo's attitude had become more and more bitter and was creating issues that upset the other artisans. I tried to use disciplinary tactics and letters of reprimand that went in his employment files. I told him his attitude needed to change and even threatened to fire him. Nothing changed. He seemed to always have a chip on his shoulder — and I couldn't figure out where that chip came from. Yet he was one of our smartest and most talented employees. I really didn't want to lose him.

Angelo had been born with a childhood disease. His illness had left him bedridden and a burden to his parents. His dad had chosen not to give Angelo his legal last name, assuming he would not make it to adulthood, and his dad had even told Angelo's mother to just let him die. The medical burdens were too much. His mom refused. As a result, Angelo became the only one of his siblings who carried his mother's maiden name as a surname. As he approached his teens, something changed, and Angelo's body healed itself. Angelo is today by all standards normal. I am astonished that he is such a quick thinker and so talented, given his history. I confessed to him that I was amazed at what he had endured as a child. But despite my admiration for his overcoming his upbringing, he certainly had not been freed from the emotional scars.

I sat him down on multiple occasions and we talked about his attitude toward life. It seemed apparent to me that the bitterness he had for his father was poisoning his heart and pervading all aspects of his life — including work. I told him he needed to let it go. I knew that all his potential would be wasted by his bad attitude and entitled behavior. I tried to explain all of this to him as well. Angelo and I had a bumpy relationship for years. His attitude continued to be toxic in our work environment, and I finally caved in and decided to let him go.

I had a meeting with my Haitian director. Deciding to fire a worker is no small matter. Besides the legal paperwork, severance pay, and possibility of being taken to court, the ramifications are heavy. Given that the artisan has nothing to lose, firing an employee often becomes an ordeal for the employer. We have even caught someone stealing red-handed, but didn't mention it as the reason they were being fired because a counter-attack suit for defamation of character isn't worth the risk. Even if all goes smoothly, the fact that they are losing the only source of income they have, and their children might starve, makes it a heavy and heart-wrenching decision. We went back and forth on the options. What kind of severance pay would we owe him? Who would replace him? As frustrating as he had become to work with, his intelligence had made him an asset to the team that would be sorely missed.

The night before we were going to give him notice, I felt a nudge that I would say was from God. It happens from time to time that I get a gut feeling telling me to do something that doesn't make sense. I have learned that I need to listen to that gut, even if it does seem counterintuitive. That day, that holy whisper told me to do something quite the opposite of anything that made sense.

I had the wild idea to promote him.

What? I thought. Promote him? For what? He has been a pain in the neck for years. The last thing he needed was a promotion to further inflate his ego and cocky attitude!

"Promote him," it whispered again. "He needs to feel valued."

I wrestled with this all night. The next day, I approached my director.

"Junior," I said, sheepishly. "What if we give Angelo a significant raise and a clear new job description for a promotion?"

Junior looked down at me over his glasses.

"I know it sounds crazy," I said, "but I think that Angelo needs to feel more a part of the team. I think he needs to feel like he is valued more and appreciated for the work he does. Can we just try it as an experiment and see what happens? I mean, worst case scenario is that we let him go in two months if nothing changes. No loss on our end."

Junior, who was always reluctantly tolerant of my hare-brained ideas, gave me a look that said he would put up with me this time. We both really wanted to see a good resolution. Neither one of us wanted to see Angelo suffer. He agreed to join me in my experiment.

In his new role, we opened the company books to Angelo that month, so that he had a deeper understanding and insight into the company's behind-the-scenes struggles. The raise and promotion also followed as promised. For the next two weeks, we treated him as an equal on the senior management team. We opened his eyes to an understanding of who we were as a company and what we were trying to accomplish. He could now clearly see our roadblocks and what we struggled with financially.

It was transformative.

It worked.

Angelo was never the same. He remains with us to this day as one of our most valuable and esteemed employees. He is an advocate for the company amongst the other employees; he is humble; he is grateful; and he is very loved. Angelo became a different person on the day he felt valued.

My upside-down strategy for promotion worked. It was a crazy idea that panned out. A promotion with clear expectations and giving value to people does wonders for their work ethic and makes their spirits soar. Being transparent about our business pains and having transparency with our managers is something we value as a company. We feel that the more under-standing they have in our world, the more of a team player they become.

* * *

My faith plays into my decisions about how to handle the hurt-ing situations around me. I know in my own life I have so far to go and grow in my own healing and in my own transformation. The grace that has been shown to me compels me to see those I work with in this same light. It is difficult to run a business as a boss and as a Christ-follower called to love. My decisions do not always convey the love of God — and yet I know that the balance of both is what I am called to. It is a tightrope I walk and fall from every day.

2. Loving the Unlovely

*J*aqueline came running at full speed toward my home gate. She was screaming.

"Open the gate! Open the gate!"

The security guard cracked the door and peered outside as Jaqueline threw her full body weight against the door. It caught him off balance and she forced her way past him to the safety of the artisan house.

Stunned, the security guard had to quickly regain his senses, because someone was running right behind Jaqueline. Not wanting to be outdone again, he braced himself and held the door steady. The man chasing Jaqueline was irate. He cursed out the security guard and demanded to be let in. But Jaqueline worked here. Her husband did not. The security guard denied him entry.

Jaqueline stood panting, safely inside, halfway bent over and trying to catch her breath, and words started to tumble out of her mouth. Her left eye was split open and swollen.

"I was out buying groceries at the market this afternoon." Deep breaths. "I was supposed to be home just before the kids got home from school. But the tap-tap coming home got a flat tire and we all got stranded in traffic. All the tap-taps were full, and it took me a while to get another with space to bring me back to our area. By the time I got home he was already irate. He thought I had been with another man. He started yelling at me. Grabbed me to try to check my phone. I had been out of minutes, so I wasn't able to call him. When he reached for me I fell back-wards and hit my head."

It was then I noticed the gooey blood down the back of her head and on the back of her dress.

"I screamed at him," she continued, "and cursed him, and I bit him on the arm as he reached for my phone. I hadn't done anything wrong, and I wasn't going to let him take my phone."

She bit him, and he lashed out at her with a clenched fist. The crack of his hand hitting her face and her howling brought a crowd of neighbors out to watch the scuffle. Several women entered their home to try to get him off her. The interruption al-lowed Jaqueline the moment she needed to scramble to her feet and bolt out the door. She ran as fast as her legs could carry her, knowing he would be right behind. He had nearly caught up when she got to the gate. For now, she was safe.

It turned out her husband had been home all day. He was unemployed and unable to contribute to the family income through work, so he resorted to amusing himself during the day playing dominos and drinking with his friends. This afternoon he had drank too much and overreacted with rage.

Jacqueline had just started working with us rolling beads and was successful at it. The balance of power had shifted in her home, as she was bringing home the daily wages and he felt less secure of his position as head of the household. Alcohol and embarrassment are a bad combination.

I didn't know Jaqueline well yet, but I was not liking her husband. It wasn't the first time one of our artisans had come to work beaten and I was tiring of seeing our women artisans subjected to abuse. My culture has rightfully ingrained it into me that that is a vile behavior. In America, domestic violence might be a silent epidemic, but in Haiti it is much more out in the open.

Over the next week we had a lot of discussion in our workplace about domestic violence. It goes both ways, unfortunately. Men often strike their wives with physical force and admit it. But a glance at their arms will often tell a tale of abuse toward them as well. For women, the weapon of choice seems to be their teeth, and I have a fair share of artisan men with bitemark-shaped scars up and down their arms.

Sitting in a circle and discussing the situations Haitian women find themselves in has brought so much enlightenment. They come at things from such a different vantage point than I would.

Denise was the most outspoken. Years earlier she had begun working for Papillon and had quickly advanced to become a manager. She was called "Soer Denise" (Sister Denise) by all the other artisans — a term of respect given to churchgoers who try to live to a higher standard.

She began her story. "I was once like Jaqueline. My husband used to beat me so badly daily. He was so angry and stressed out by money. I couldn't contribute financially and any time I would ask for money to go buy food, he would get angry and beat me. I became so afraid of him that I wanted to leave. Knowing this, he threatened that he would kill me if I left. I stayed, and I cowered every time I saw him." Her face had scars on it that verified her story.

"Finally," she continued, "I found this job rolling beads and started making some money. I stopped having to ask him for money every time I needed to go to the market and so his stress was relieved. He was much happier. When I got promoted to manager, I started making even more money. I bought the little plot of land next door to our house and started buying bricks and building a home one brick at a time. After work, I would come home, and we would talk about what we were going to do with our money and what we should do next in the house we are building.

"One day I came home late from work. I hadn't let him know where I was, and he was angry at me. When I walked in the door he started yelling and he raised his hand to hit me. It had been a while. He stopped suddenly and put his hand down and went and sat down on the bed.

"I stood in the middle of the room with my arms crossed and I looked at him and I said, 'I don't need you for your money anymore. Don't ever hit me again.' To this day, he has never hit me. I feel like having a job gave me a choice to stand up for myself. Now he needs my money and he knows he can't treat me like that anymore."

Domestic abuse is wrong for sure, but with no alternate models and with children being raised by parents who are physically harmful to each other, little boys and girls grow up to do the same. A measure of grace must be extended and an attempt to educate alternative conflict resolution must be offered before a person is completely vilified for this kind of behavior. Somehow most of these couples seem to get over their grievances and work things out.

A year later Jacqueline approached me and asked if she could speak to me privately. She had a favor she wanted to ask.

"Shelley, I am earning money and am so grateful for a job, but I still am not making enough and was wondering if you could perhaps give my husband a job."

I still had judgment in my heart. No way, I thought. I don't give wife beaters jobs. My heart was slightly softened by the look in her eyes. Giving her husband a job would help her. In many ways, it was the lack of dignity and the boredom that led to the drinking that caused his outbursts.

She pleaded with me further, "Please, Shelley, he can work in the clay department. He is good at manual labor and will work hard for you. If you do this, we can afford to send our two boys to a better school and they will have a better chance in the future."

I still wasn't convinced. I told her no and left it at that. I wanted to reserve space in our workforce for women who were in desperate need. But I was also, in that moment, convinced that it was not my place to be the judge. I too had made mistakes and received multiple do-overs in my life. Who knows where I would be in life if I hadn't been given the opportunity that I was born into? A year passed and Jaqueline continued to work and do well. One day there was a knock at the office door and Jaqueline poked her head in with a look of despair in her eyes. She was short of breath and asking for medical help. A quick look at her swollen ankles showed that the blood was having a hard time making its way back up to her heart. After a few calls to some medical professional friends of mind, we realized that she was experiencing heart failure. I will never forget the moment with her, sitting on the couch in my office, touching her terrified face as the tears streamed down, knowing she was most likely about to leave her two small boys behind. She died only two days later. There was nothing we could do. She was in her thirties and I mourned the fact that had she lived in another country, she might have had a chance to live. She might have been able to see her kids grow up. It doesn't seem fair.

After I found out about her death, my thoughts immediately went to her children. I decided to walk down to the one-room cinder block home where she had lived. Her sister and her husband were in the house in mourning. Her two boys were sitting on the bed stunned by the sudden loss of their mother. I asked the family what their plan was. How were they going to take care of the boys?

They stared at me blankly. "We don't have any way to take care of them. We don't have jobs."

I was conflicted. I had been so angry with her husband for what he had done to her in the past, but I was concerned more for the boys and them getting their daily needs met. I decided to finally set aside my judgement and offered them both jobs on the spot.

I came back to the office looking for affirmation from my Haitian director, who was responsible for discipline issues in the workplace.

"What do you think, Junior? I mean, I really didn't want to give him a job...but..."

He raised his eyebrows and affirmed my concerns.

"I know you don't like how he has treated her, but this might just be the only way to help her boys."

Jaqueline's husband started in the clay department and works processing clay to this day. After he was hired, he stopped drinking and focused his attention on raising his boys well. He never caused any problems and continued to provide well for his boys.

He taught me and continues to teach me a huge lesson about grace, opportunity, and judgment. Who knows whether it would have been the same outcome had I hired him before her death. But I was glad that grace won in this situation.

I do have regrets that Jaqueline never got to see the dignity with which her husband conducted himself after her passing. But I am forever grateful that her sons were able to have a father who was willing and able to provide for them as they grew. Perhaps they were able to see a different father because he had the dignity of work instead of the one who would have otherwise raised them. This past year Jaqueline's husband fell ill. He would come to work and have no bladder control and would soil himself at work. Still, he very rarely missed work. We paid for treatment for him through our nonprofit Papillon Empowerment, but it was to no avail. He was getting weaker. The last time I saw him, he thanked me for all I had done for his family. They knew he was dying and eventually the family took him out to the countryside to pass away. The boys are on my radar. They are now double orphans in need of sponsorship for school. If you would like to help them or kids like them, please feel free to donate to Papillon Empowerment to allow us to facilitate funding distribution.

3. Domestic Adoption as a Solution

A man in his sixties sat across the living room from me in his La-Z-Boy rocking chair. His hair was a little unkempt, his eyes kind, his glasses a little low on his nose. In his arms he held a tiny bundle, barely a week old. He looked like a new grandfather and certainly acted like one the way his love poured out over the baby girl in his arms. I was in Olympia, Washington, and had heard about this remarkable couple and had invited myself over.

All of a sudden the infant started to tremble. He held her tight and rubbed her back.

"That's the effects of coming down off the drugs," he said as he glanced at his wife who sat across the room in a rocking chair playing with a six-month-old baby girl with big brown eyes. That baby was also suffering from withdrawal symptoms.

As I glanced her way, my eyes locked on those brown eyes and her big smile erupted showing two bottom teeth just coming in. She was beautiful and perfect in every way. She had been with her foster family since birth.

In my attempts to find good solutions to the adoption crisis, I had decided to seek out people who were doing orphan care well locally. The couple who invited me into their home had been doing foster care for decades and their niche was drug-dependent babies. Over the course of the years, they had adopted six children, but now that they were getting older, they had committed to be a loving yet temporary receiving home for babies who desperately needed a safe place as they entered the world.

"The need is so great," he said, and his wife agreed.

"When it's time for one to leave," she said, "and the social worker comes to pick them up, they will often have another in the car ready to drop off with us. It is a revolving door of babies around here." She added, "We can only take two at a time. But we always have two. Always."

I shook my head in disbelief.

Most men and women in their sixties are playing golf and going on cruises, or at least relaxing and watching TV. These two were holding babies and loving them through drug withdrawals and staying up all night changing diapers and warming bottles. Where do people like this come from? There certainly aren't enough of them in this world.

"Why don't more people do what you do?" I asked. The babies struck a nerve in my soul. It was hard to walk away not inspired to do something. But the reality is what everyone knows is going to happen.

"People are afraid of getting their hearts broken," she said. "You love a baby and then you have to give them back knowing that they may not ever be in a stable loving family like you know you could provide."

Tough stuff to chew on.

So, does that mean we don't do it? I thought. Because it's hard? Leave a baby at the hospital to go through withdrawal all alone?

She and her husband talked about how the government's goal is always family reunification first, but with the babies they care for, they see very few success stories. They attribute this to the fact that drug dependency is part of the equation. Most of their babies are in and out of foster care throughout their whole childhoods.

Heartbreaking. I have spent my life talking about family preservation, and yet this seems like such another stark shade of grey. How can we make this right? It seems so unfair for the children born into this.

Like Haiti itself, it can be overwhelming if you look at the enormity of the problem. It feels like no matter how you might try, you can never make a real difference. The systems are so greatly flawed. But a gentle grandpa holding a tiny baby in his arms and rocking her through her pain showed me that his kindness was making a difference in that moment.

Most people who give to orphanages abroad do so out of a call from their conscience and their faith. They believe that they are supposed to take care of orphans in this world. And yet here in America we have a tremendous need within our very own foster care system. We overlook it for many reasons. Maybe it isn't as glamorous. Maybe we think it will hurt more. But the truth is that if we really believe in orphan care, we need to invest as much in care and prevention in our own country as we do abroad.

My friends told me about how the foster-to-adopt program is affordable, has financial aid, medical help, even scholarship for university available for families willing to adopt. Foster care may have some challenges. Home studies and social workers can be invasive, kids can have baggage, you may even get your heart broken by tiny babies whom you get attached to, but truth be told, that is not all that different than challenges of international adoption.

Most families who have adopted or fostered go through emotional trauma that the outsider knows nothing about. It's true that you don't know what I'm talking about until you are an adoptive parent or have a special needs child. Believe me when I say these parents need a break. Children from hard places carry pain that you, as their parent, have to live with and manage. My own son has an eating disorder, a learning disability, and behavioral issues that have broken my heart over and over again. It's not his fault that he is hurt but it is sometimes exhausting to parent him. Foster and adoptive parents need help! They need to go on a date as a couple. They need to have a meal brought over. They need some basic groceries brought in. They have a lot of kids and probably aren't rich and could use some clothes for their kids, or diapers, or formula.

But they will probably never ask for help.

The solution? Help anyway. Loving on adoptive parents and foster parents IS orphan care. Leave the diapers on the doorstep. Or the groceries. Bring over the meal. Find out what size shoes their kids need and just go buy some shoes.

Many adoptive and foster parents deal with behavioral issues that can cause so much emotional trauma the parents want to curl up and hide. They can't reach out. Few people understand them. It may be all they can do to take care of their family. Be gracious and be supportive. By being a support to an adoptive family, you in turn are a part of the orphan care solution in the world. Adopt an adoptive family, so to speak. Be their biggest cheerleaders.

4. Better Lovers of the World

A couple of visitors came into the boutique in Haiti to buy some souvenirs, and I ended up striking up a conversation. Trying to be friendly, I asked them what they did the week that they were in Haiti.

They stared at the floor and started to fidget.

An awkward silence ensued.

Eventually, the woman muttered that she had been volunteering at a local orphanage and she immediately followed her statement with a string of explanations.

"We know how you feel about orphanages."

"We just wanted to bring milk for the babies."

"We didn't hardly spend any time really."

Their confessions were fluid and the defenses were up.

I want to be clear when I say that, as strongly as I feel that children should not be raised in orphanages, I am not the judge of the world of missions. Orphanages are often necessary because of a crisis or because it was already established before the current directors took over to do their best with the kids who are there. I am not going to stand in judgment over anyone. My hope is that we just all start asking the critical questions and move toward better practices, always for the sake of the poor and the children.

When I was a child, one of my favorite things to do was to visit pet stores. There was always a lineup of puppies, and sometimes they would even let you hold the puppies and play with them. Times have changed, and we realize that dogs were not being treated well in the puppy mill industry. I loved spending my time with those puppies, but also understand why it is rare to find them in pet stores anymore. I am so thankful that we are a people who can realize how to do things better and change.

It is my hope that someday orphanages also become a thing of the past. Because we know better. Because we know the children for the most part aren't really orphans. And because we become a part of the solution to the root of the problem and buy into the idea of job creation and education as better alternatives.

But when a crisis does occur, or a country is too poor to handle their children born with challenges, far be it from me to stand in judgment when the situations within a crisis framework call for desperate measures to keep children alive. An orphanage in this context might be the most loving and realistic solution.

5. Scarcity Mentality

*B*efore I conclude, I can't help but talk about guilt. Working with the poor subjects a person to a strong array of emotions. The most poignant in my experience is guilt. Questions bombard you as you move through your day. Why was I born into privilege? What gives me the right to have when others don't? Why should they suffer and even die because of where they were born? Particularly the children get to us. We want to wrap them all up and take them home with us because we acknowledge that we have a blessing that they were not born into.

But where does the guilt come from and how does it help us serve the poor? Our first instinct may be to imagine giving away everything we have in order to alleviate the suffering of the poor. We feel somehow as if we are not worthy of such privilege. But even if we gave all we had to the poor, how much better off would they be in a week, or a month, or a year? Would that solve the problem? Some of us are called to extreme poverty. I commend those who are. But I would also argue that living a life of intentional poverty, though it might alleviate guilt and give better understanding, does not help the poor or relieve their suffering.

Pity often goes hand in hand with guilt. As innocent as it seems, pity only serves to cripple the poor even further. Lavish handouts create dependency. A misunderstanding of the fact that the poor also have assets and economies that we know nothing about keeps us wringing our hands and feeling sorry for them. I watch Haitian school children coming home from school in their uniforms bouncing along the dusty trails and talking with their friends only to get home, shed their formal uniforms, get into their play clothes that look like rags to us and start a fierce game of soccer in the open fields. They are free and they are happy. When they have the opportunity for education and are well fed, they do pretty well. What looks to us, with our U.S. viewpoint, to be an unhappy life, can in fact be extremely happy. It's just different from what we grew up with and what we expect.

Pity is not the right reaction. It is degrading and demeaning. Empathy and wanting to empower is the right reaction. We don't need to be poor ourselves to solve the problem of poverty in the world. We just have to invite them into the opportunity that we ourselves have experienced. Jobs and education are the most practical solutions. The world's economy is not a fixed number. It isn't a certain size that we have to divvy up to make sure everyone gets an equal amount. It has the ability to expand. We can fight to see others rise to meet us where we are. And our place of privilege gets leveraged as a blessing for others. I don't have to feel guilty that I have a car and a house and a computer and food. Rather I make sure to use my resources with the economically disadvantaged in mind. How can I use what I have to increase opportunity in their lives so that they eventually can rise to where I am blessed to be?

6. A Final Word

I came to Haiti with the hope of doing what what was expected of a short term missions trip to a poor country — hold babies, give hand-outs, and help alleviate the suffering I saw there. A decade later, I feel strongly that the best way to alleviate poverty is to create sustainable opportunities that go far beyond a handout. But even within solutions such as education, job creation, and training, there are so many issues to be addressed and to be aware of!

I am continually faced with a choice to love in spite of my inability to fix things. Consider the ladies who wait at the gate of my business day after day pleading for a job. They stand in the hot sun waiting for me to come out so they can run up and grab my attention, hoping I will listen to their plight. They too want the chance to provide for their families. Unfortunately, jobs are also a truly scarce resource.

Since I don't have nearly as many positions to give as there is need, I have a decision to make. Do I rush by the women as quickly as possible, hoping to avoid the terrible pleas for help that I can't satisfy? Frankly, it's what I want to do, because my heart can't handle the sound of desperation. My heart can't handle saying "no, no, no" to the moms who deserve a chance.

Then something bigger in me, my conscience, tells me to stop and see them. Give them recognition, Shelley. Take the time to listen, even for five minutes. Apologize that you can't help. Let them know they are seen. Recognize the humanity in everyone, even if that is all you can do.

The ladies listen when I ask them to hold onto hope, to not give up. I tell them to pray for God's blessing. I tell them to pray for me and for the business, because if Papillon grows, then I may have a chance to hire more people. I wonder, sometimes, if this might just be the secret to the success that Papillon has had in Haiti — an army of poor desperate mothers standing outside all day, praying. When taking the time to see them, I feel a connection to my greater purpose in this world. To love people. Perhaps, in an endless ocean of needy people looking out for themselves, they haven't felt much care and concern for their own well-being. Maybe in those small moments in my front yard I can fill up a need as deep as their need for money. I won't pretend you can live on love alone, but I do believe that it is an overlooked asset that I am learning how to tap into more.

I think about our other everyday worlds. In America, I walk by a homeless, heroin-addicted young woman begging for money. Do I really see her? Do I make her feel like she has value? The food server who doesn't bring me my food on time, the car sales rep who is just hustling a sale. What is the back story and how can we love them better?

My humanitarian tendencies keep me focused on the physical needs of people around me, but it's important to remember in the world of charity that when the money dries up and the donations and sales go away, we still have an endless supply of a very needed gift to give that never runs dry. Our love is free and is needed.

Working in service of others is tough. The honeymoon phase with the poor ends quickly and imperfections become more and more transparent to a point that it can make you question yourself entirely! Should I help a man who beats his wife? Or a mom who neglects her kids? Or a mom who gives her child away?

My answer is yes.

In my opinion, being good or perfect isn't what determines one's value or makes them worthy of being extended a hand. And maybe supporting an organization or business with flaws is alright, too. Maybe even someone like me, divorced and with my own issues I continue to work through, is still trying to help as much as she can. It's good news! It means we are all qualified to help and be helped, no matter how broken we all are.

Maybe the sheer act of staying engaged can be the catalyst to bring wholeness to a situation.

The business of working with the poor is not a fairy tale story. Many times, it ends badly.

But it is still worth it. No matter what.

Because people are worth it.

And a mom standing outside the gate holding her baby is worth it.

This is the Orphan Gospel.

That she might be able to keep her baby.

That her baby might have a chance to stay with its mother.

Orphan Gospel
Discussion Questions

Section 1 Questions
The Poor Will Always Be With You:
Understanding Systemic Poverty

- Do you know someone who seems like they were "set up" for failure in life?

- Is it fair to consider their history? How does understanding it help?

- Imagine yourself in their story. Would you want opportunity, pity, charity, or something else?

- How can we be more humble in our dealings with the poor, the drug addicted, the mentally ill, or other marginalized people?

- How can we better understand the struggle they face?

- What is the difference between empathy and understanding and pity?

- What kinds of things do we do in a pity response? What kinds of things do we do in an empathetic response?

Section 2 Questions
Go Into All the World:
The Heart of Missions

- How do we keep the gospel authentic when working with the poor? How have you seen it done badly?

- How do we not make the gospel about the thing they are receiving?

- Are we more responsible for spiritual care or for meeting people's physical needs?

- What is the difference? How can we do well at both?

- Is creating opportunity also meeting a legitimate need?

Section 3 Questions
I Will Not Leave You as Orphans:
The Poverty Orphan

- What are some of the misconceptions you may have had about orphans?

- Have you ever heard someone talk about wanting to take an orphan home with them after their mission's trip?

- How often do you hear talk about the parents of children in orphanages?

- What are our thoughts about the family units of poor children?

Section 4 Questions
Good News to the Poor:
Creating Jobs as a Holy Practice

- Why is job creation not often thought of as a Biblical way to help the poor?

- What would your biggest challenge be in starting a work initiative with the poor?

- How can you contribute to jobs in poor communities from where you are?

- Why is giving a job a more sustainable way to help?

Section 5 Questions
Innocent as Doves, Wise as Serpents:
Cultural Considerations

- What cultural assumptions do you have about the poor that you might need to change or question?

- Have you ever assumed that you are more successful in life because you are smarter? How much does opportunity play a role in your success?

- How can you ensure quality education in the schools you support in poor communities?

- Have you sponsored a child? If so, have you investigated the school's teaching methods?

Section 6 Questions
Be the Good News Where You Are:
Living Out Heaven on Earth

- Have you ever experienced the need to do the opposite of what was expected and it somehow worked out?

- Does God have a say? Does He lead us to know what to do in baffling circumstances?

- How does grace fit in to caring for the poor?

- How much is really black and white?

- How can we be a part of the solution for orphan prevention both internationally and at home?

- Do you feel like orphanages are the best way to help children? When are they necessary?